MW01601189

Book Cover by Fred Hilgenfeldt

Illustrations by Fred Hilgenfeldt

First edition, 2024

Contents

Preface

I want to take you on a journey. A journey through mountains as steep and tall and valleys as far and wide as the human mind can imagine. A journey full of despair, humility and laughter. I want to invite you to ponder topics like...

- experiences

- emotions

- healing

- identity

- purpose

- authenticity

- acceptance

- gratitude

- responsibility

- love

- character

- serenity

- discipline

- purpose

In the last 15 years, I have spent a great deal of my time thinking about these topics and trying to deal with them. Now, for you as much as for myself, I want to put my findings all together in one place. I hope this book inspires you to live the life you want. Or to learn to accept that darkness following every one of us like a shadow. Or to build stable relationships. Or to reach for the stars. I hope it inspires you to find some peace and compassion in this hell of a ride called life.

Throughout the book, I will switch back and forth between theoretical ideas and personal stories. The stories show how I relate to these ideas and how they convinced me in the first place. They contain aspects, archetypes and themes that I have come across over the course of my life. Looking back now, I wish they would have crossed my path before I turned 16. I wish they would cross everyone's path in adolescence. Learning and understanding these ideas would have saved me a lot of hardships in life. I could have sped up my never-ending journey towards maturity, stability and serenity.

I will also reference other authors and their ideas. The value lies within the distillation, combination and integration of these ideas. This should give you an overview and enable you to go into more detail for the parts that speak to you. As always with ideas - discern, take what you think is useful and leave the rest be.

Intro

Flow

F low. Everything flows. *Panta Rhei.* A small sentence with big meaning. Enough for an entire book it turns out. However, I had actually written the majority of the text by the time I realized that this is the concept that summarizes the book. It is the common denominator of psychological, philosophical and spiritual questions. Everything flows. But what did the Greek philosopher Herclitus mean with this saying? The book has been broken into four parts.

In Part I - *The Self in Resistance,* we look at patterns of learned resistance to experiences. An evolutionary bias to get stuck in traumatic experiences. These experiences can distort our perception of reality. To resolve this, we need to realize that the danger has passed and that we are completely safe. In ancient times, this focus on the negative would help us to avoid repeated confrontation of known dangers. In today's world, barely anything genuinely threatens our survival. This makes our learned focus on the negative rather unnecessary.

Part II - *The Self in Flow* is a toolbox to accessing blocked experiences and emotions and resolving them. With the tools provided, we can let experiences pass through our body and mind to feel safe. We also learn about the art of observation without judgement or blocking. Authentically expressing experiences instead of resisting them leads to a natural flow.

In Part III - *The World in Flow,* we draw inspiration from historical texts and concepts. We learn why the saying is "everything flows" instead of "I flow". We become aware of the connection between ourselves and the world. We discuss the relationship between suffering and growth. We will learn how attachment leads to suffering. We'll also discuss how a spiritual death leads us to an eternal self that is constantly unfolding as impermanent worldly ongoings. Connection, non-duality and impermanence are key concepts coming into play here. These discussions are wonderful for thinking about the big, philosophical questions in life. Unfortunately, getting stuck in theory can too often feel disconnected from our daily life.

This is why in Part IV - *The World in Action* we translate these ideas into daily life. How do we turn prior insights into a lasting quality of life? What are actionable steps that we can take along the way? We'll explore the advantages of having goals, discipline and a purpose. Moreover, we will learn about the importance of responsibility. It is crucial to find a balance between a desire for action while not being concerned with the fruit of our action. The less we worry about the resulting impact of our action, the more content we feel about the current state of affairs.

The Self in Resistance

Part I

Chapter One

Consciousness

When you experience an experience, it comes and goes,
but when you resist an experience, it persists.

Brad Blanton

It's 3 am. The foul smell of the half-smoked cigarette that I rolled and lit up an hour ago is still filling my room. I forgot about it, distracted by the games I'm playing on the computer. It's now waiting to be smoked to the bitter end, lying in my ashtray. The wooden ashtray looks like a tiny version of a Filipino bungalow on the beach. Whatever emotions are floating around in my (sub-)consciousness - I don't want to listen to them. I don't want to know. I didn't even want to commit my attention to a whole cigarette away from playing on the computer. For thirty minutes at a time, I am completely submerged in steering my character to victory. The emotions that this confronts me with, I can deal with. Rage about (supposedly) incompetent teammates. Pride about victory. I am focused on the game and forget everything else around me. I forget that I have an exam at university in about six hours, that I should probably start studying for at some point. I forget that I had 4 months' worth of time to prepare for this week of exams. And I forget that this is not even my first go at a successful semester at university. Actually, it's my fourth. When I started university more than two years ago, my plan was to treat it like my school career. I wanted to dispose of it as quickly and with as little effort as humanly possible. This plan lasted for... about three months. From then it started going downhill. Thinking about it now, three months is actually surprisingly long, considering how bad of a plan it was to begin with.

Why didn't I start sooner? I had the whole day. Heck, I had the whole month. Why was I not able to just do it? The word failure comes to mind. "Great potential, but a lost cause" my tombstone would read. I always did have a tendency for being dramatic. However, failure would imply that I missed something I aimed at, wouldn't it? Not having to study for an exam appeared to be more important for me than getting anywhere in life. I didn't have any intrinsic motivation for studying or getting my degree. My rather naive vision had been confronted and burst by reality a long time ago. It had been a vision of humanity that was organized in subsistence and community life. So what am I still even studying for? What do I want to do with my life? Sometimes, the dragons of chaos in your life have to get so big until you have no other choice than to face them. To start asking yourself the right questions. To be conscious of what's going on in your life. In this case, consciousness helped me to become aware of the problems in my life. It was the first prerequisite for change and improvement

Consciousness is what differentiates us as a species on this planet. It enabled us to reach the top of the food chain in the evolutionary blink of an eye. It is also what enables you to further evolve and "differentiate" yourself from your past self. It is the torch that shines light on your problems. It helps you realize useful next steps and it opens the channel to meditational awareness. We can summarize the essence of Buddha's teachings by his quote:"love yourself and observe". Consciousness or observational awareness covers the second and in my opinion much more important half of this.

Do not quote Buddha. Be Buddha.

Buddha

Just kidding. Here is a better quote:

Neuroscience research shows that the only way we can change the way we feel is by becoming aware of our inner experience and learning to befriend what is going inside ourselves.

Bessel van der Kolk

Consciousness will be the enabler for most other themes you will find in this book. A lot of them have to do with becoming aware of certain patterns in your life. Osho even goes so far as to say that consciousness itself is enough to heal and solve things. He was a spiritual teacher who brought Eastern philosophies to the Western world in the eighties.

Nathaniel Brandon considers "the practice of living consciously" to be the first of the six core pillars on the way to high self-esteem. He is regarded as one of the main authorities on self-esteem. Our species has the unique ability to make a conscious decision if we want to seek awareness or if we want to avoid it. This is crucial for our development, as a species as much as an individual. It is also important for managing life and its ongoing tasks and challenges. Think of situations where you are thinking along the lines of: *I know... but.....*

- I know I should start studying, but I just don't really want to right now.

- I know I should think about how I could achieve more at university or in general, but I can still do it tomorrow. Right now there is no harm in watching a series or playing on the computer for a while, is there?

- I know my children should get to spend more time with me, but work is just so demanding right now.

- I know I've been having problems with my partner, but we are probably just going through a bad phase.

- I know I'm currently drinking a lot/spending a lot/taking drugs, but so what? I don't see the issue, I could easily stop if I wanted.

- I know there is a pesky task at work but somehow I just don't get around to doing it.

If we don't face tough situations, they will grow and wreak havoc in our lives. Look at the problems listed above and think of their potential consequences. Kids who feel ignored. Divorce, or remaining in unhappy relationships. Alcoholism. Falling into debt. Not doing well at work.

*We cannot feel competent and worthy while conducting
our lives in a mental fog.*

Nathaniel Branden

To underline this thought, I want to make a quick reference to a writing exercise that Jordan B. Peterson uses in his Maps of Meaning program. The program supports adolescents in finding a sense of belonging in the world. People generally have a good idea of how their life would go wrong if it went wrong. Take about 20 minutes and think of all problems in your life where you might find it difficult to confront them. Your weaknesses, your foolishness, your possible inadequacies. And then imagine what your life would be like, if you allowed them to have the upper hand. This should give you reason enough to bring up appropriate discipline and the courage to face these problems. In Part IV - *The World in Action*, we will look at an actual positive future to aim at.

Of course you don't always need to have a super high level of awareness for everything that is going on around you. It is in the evolutionary nature of our being that feeling safe will decrease our adrenaline, stress hormones and focus. It simply saves energy to only process as much information as currently needed to survive or find food. It is more about having an appropriate level of focus for whatever is going on in your life.

Unfortunately, I didn't do this exercise before I started going to university in the fall of 2010. It took me more than two years of a car crash in slow motion to illustrate to myself in real life what happens when I let my dragons have the upper hand. I was tiptoeing back and forth between looking at a screen, being drunk or sleeping. The most important thing to me was to not be conscious, because I was so afraid of what I would stumble upon, once I started looking. I knew I had to change something. I couldn't keep going on like this. So, I made the decision to move away from Vienna and spent my days working in landscaping. When you spend ten hours a day, six days a week mowing lawns, pulling weeds and shoveling truckloads of gravel by hand, you have plenty of time where your mind is unoccupied. Luckily, I became conscious of my life and my problems. It wasn't about the big picture yet. It was about finding a modus operandi that works for me. The day starts, so I get up in the morning and do something. I have goals. I work towards them. I am aware of the general trajectory of my life and my actions. I eventually ended up moving back to Vienna and finding a room that was situated less than 10 minutes by foot away from university, despite being away from the city center and away from friends. I wanted to keep the hurdles to productivity and achievement as low as possible. Only after the first year, when I had more or less successfully established good habits of working and going to university, did I move to a more central district. I

managed to finish the (large) remaining part of my undergrad within two years of returning.

Increasing awareness

So how exactly can we recognize and create a high level of consciousness and awareness? There are several things that we can observe and do in this direction. We can create a specific time and space in our diary to let our thoughts wander freely or follow a set of questions. For example, every Thursday night from 8pm to 10pm. This includes introducing safety barriers to prevent distraction from your phone, computer, TV or friends and family. The only thing with you at this time should be a pen and paper to catch whatever is going on inside your head.

Great thinkers like Einstein and Nietzsche had time to be "lost in their minds" embedded in their daily routines. They liked taking long walks to work or strolling through nature for hours. Not to mention spiritual leaders who spend half their lives pondering the questions of existence with little distraction. Since you are probably neither an iconic spiritual leader, nor planning to revolutionize society's understanding of physics, you might be wondering how to break this down for your own life. Well, I consider the main goal of this exercise to be threefold:

- gaining an understanding of where you are in life,

- where you want to be and

- how you are planning on closing this gap.

This might include a possible career path, reaching milestones in your hobbies or increasing the quality of your relationships. Possible questions to ask yourself could include:

- Am I passionate about what I'm doing, or am I just in the passenger seat of my life?

- Am I generally content with my current life regarding my career, social circle and my hobbies?

- Does what I do align with my strengths and interests? (everyone has strong qualities, don't let anyone tell you otherwise!)

- What do I want my life in X years to look like? This could be about your social situation, your material well-being or your physical surroundings.

- Am I on track to achieve my goals? Do I still want to achieve those goals? Is there anything I can do to speed up the process?

- What are potential hurdles or opportunities that I might be missing?

- Am I staying true to my inner needs, thoughts and feelings? Am I expressing them where relevant?

- How do I feel about recent developments in my life?

Another way to do this, is to write a vision diary as specific as possible that you read through and update regularly. (We will go into the specifics of goals and goal setting in Part 4.)

Think about it: we have the power to consciously decide if we want to focus on something, or if we want to distract ourselves. That is incredible! Just take a moment to let it sink in! We are able to make a decision to evolve, to increase our quality of life and to change this world for the better, or to just keep ourselves busy. And surely, there are habits, emotions and (a lack of) discipline playing into it. But at the end of the day, it is you who makes the call between sitting on the couch and watching TV five nights after work, or spending the time working on something meaningful. And to prevent misunderstandings: I think that resting and playing are very important for well-being in life. But oftentimes we are just looking for what feels easiest in the moment, instead of thinking about the long-term effects. Imagine that just once or twice a week, you are going for a leisurely stroll instead of watching TV or an episode of your regular show. And while doing so, you think about the awareness questions shown above. Think of the difference this could make in just a year! You could pick up a hobby that fulfills you, have a better understanding of your purpose, or improve your relationships - instead of floating around like an astronaut in space that has lost connection to their ship.

Physical observation of yourself and your surroundings is equally important, as what you can observe in yourself usually tells you a great deal about the questions above. Your body generally mirrors emotions and emotional patterns. Have you ever paid attention to how certain emotions feel in your body? Funnily enough, you can even find them in cliché descriptions and everyday sayings, like with a *heavy heart* or *butterflies in your stomach*.

Without focusing too much on emotions that might currently be present in your life, you can also make the space to sit down and observe yourself and your body generally. Become aware of the pressure of the body resting on different points, the rhythm of breathing, the feeling of air entering your lungs, or your general blood circulation throughout your body. You can actually *feel* life going on inside your body. With regular practice, realizing that there is you as an observer and your body as the observed will create a deep and strong feeling of calmness. As a next step, physical observation can also include observation of feelings and of thoughts. It can also be conducted during mundane daily activities, like walking, speaking or working.

> *Through observation comes self-knowledge, through knowledge of self, a knowledge which reaches infinity beyond man*

Maieutique, perspective 4

More information on this will follow in Part 3 - *The World in Flow*. For now it is only important to be aware of this as a possible means to increase consciousness.

If you have experienced strong trauma in your life, increasing awareness of processes in your body can be overwhelming and possibly lead to re-traumatization. In this case, I recommend to work on these problems with professional support before you can safely increase your level of consciousness. Parts 1 and 2 of the book might help you better understand these problems and give you an indication of where to look for such support.

Addictions

Addictions, for example to drugs, alcohol, gambling or other destructive behaviors, are always a matter of suppressing consciousness in one form or another. If I know of the impact that alcohol abuse can have on a family because I have seen it first hand, and I am still drinking six nights a week, then I must have turned down awareness to a certain degree.

If I spend my nights playing on the computer, despite exams coming up, I must have turned down awareness to a certain degree. The addictive behavior itself is designed to distract you from something that you want to avoid. It might also suppress something that you feel overwhelmed by. It is essentially an extreme version of the *"avoiding uncomfortable situations"* described earlier.

Accepting your destructive behavioral patterns can be a first step towards higher awareness. This means recognizing their existence and moving them into the "scope" of your consciousness. Maybe I am currently drinking six nights a week. Maybe I am in a relationship that is detrimental for my dignity [replace with any other addictive, destructive behavior]. If you have not accepted something as status quo, it will be impossible to change or to heal. Once you have accepted something as being *real*, you can then start to *understand* it. What feelings or facts are you trying to avoid? What are the triggers that cause you to resort to such behaviors? How does it make you feel to live out this pattern?

I consider psychological addictions to be mere symptoms of deeper, structural underlying problems of how you consciously and subconsciously view yourself and the world. We will deal with the solving and healing of these problems in Part II. For now it is only helpful to be aware of the role that consciousness plays in these regards.

*One day I woke up in a hospital and someone asked me,
"What's your problem?" And I Said, "I'm an alcoholic
and an addict." And he said, "No, that's how you've
been treating your problem."*

Beautiful Boy (2018)

Nathaniel Branden uses sentence completion exercises to help his readers access subconscious knowledge and actively improve on the themes they are working on. I want to present one of these exercises here in an exemplary manner. If you feel like this matches your style of reflecting and thinking, I highly recommend spending more time with Branden's work, e.g. "the six pillars of self-esteem", "the disowned self" or "honoring the self".

This exercise should be done first thing in the morning, before doing anything else. It is about finishing a given sentence as quickly as possible, without reflecting or filtering anything that comes to mind. It's not about your output being true, useful or anything like that; the most important thing is that you write *something* that you can reflect on afterwards. Below are some examples that you can try.

To me, living consciously means...

If you have between six and ten responses written down, you can also adapt the sentence to be more specific to your situation. For example:

If I would have 5% more consciousness for the most impor-tant relationships in my life, I would...

If I would have 5% more consciousness at work, I would...

At the end of your day, last thing before you go to sleep, finish sentences of the following structure in the same manner. You can replace the topics with whatever is important for you, like relationships, work, hobbies etc.

If I thought about what I would feel like, if I would live more consciously...

If I thought about what would happen, if I would have 5% more consciousness for my tasks...

On the weekend, you can then take time to read what you wrote during the week and finish the following sentence between six and ten times:

If anything I wrote is true, then it would be helpful if I...

Keep in mind that all this should be done without any expectations and any judgement. Sessions also should not take longer than 10 minutes - it is really about accessing what is already there without any worries about the quality or outcome of what you do.

To me living consciously means...

- *Being present*

- *Feeling the body (Current emotions, tension and stress...)*

- *Perceiving and sensing without judgement*

- *Paying attention to what is required of me*

- *Not having thought loops*

- *Following an inner intuitive rhythm*

- *Feeling connected*

- *Remaining constructive*

If I would have 5% more consciousness for the most important relationships in my life I would...

- *Observe how things feel in the moment*

- *Be fully present with the person I am with*

- *Think about people's needs and how I can support them*

- *Remember more details in people's lives*

- *Take a greater interest in people's affairs*

- *Reach out to people whenever I think of them*

If anything I wrote is true It would be helpful if I...

- *Had more consciousness for the most important relationships in my life*

- *Worked on being present*

- *Focused on my breath throughout the day*

- *Observed bodily sensations and emotions arising throughout the day, without judgement*

- *Trusted intuitive needs and followed them*

- *Did what is required to stay more conscious*

Chapter Two

Emotions

*When our emotional intelligence is restricted, we often
do not know what we really want, and can consequently
struggle with even the smallest decisions*

Pete Walker[1]

You and your emotions are not the same entity. You are always
distinct from your emotional currents: there are emotions, and there
is you. You can always become aware of the existing observer in the
background, that is behind the emotions. Being conscious of this fact
is good practice to not allow emotions to take control of you. Ideally,
you want to be able to observe your emotions and their patterns so you
can understand the stories they tell you and consciously decide if and
how you act on an arising emotion. It also helps with discerning and

---

1. Pete Walker, Complex PTSD, p.41

untangling contradictory emotions that coexist. You might be grateful for what someone has done *for* you while still being angry for what they have done *to* you.

> *Hate, love, disappointment, combativeness, sadness or*
> *happiness arise in you as clouds and lightning arise in*
> *the sky. They come, they go, they develop independently*
> *from your will. Verify that. Verify that your reality lies*
> *behind all sentimental turmoils or harmonies.*

Maieutique, perspective

What is the use of emotions though? With the paragraph you have just read, you might be inclined to think that they are just unnecessary worries and one should learn to just "let them fly" and be stoic about them. However, beyond the obvious enjoyment of positive emotions, they serve a great deal of functionality. Think of emotions like a compass of your overall state of being, with different emotions posing as different directions on the compass. So for example if you are very angry, your state of being is shifting in the direction of anger on your "emotional compass". It is indicating to you that anger is between you and the balanced middle of your emotional state of being. So let's say my siblings stole my readily-prepared breakfast out of the fridge. If I had no emotional response in the form of anger, I might go about my day as if nothing happened. Subsequently, I will probably become hungry and my performance at school or work might suffer. Anger serves as an indicator that in this case, something I think I *should* have had control over was taken from me. The appropriate response might be to tell my siblings off, or if it happens again, to store my breakfast elsewhere, or - the ultima ratio - to move out and live somewhere where they don't have the ability to take my breakfast away from me. Contrary to what one might expect, the exact middle of the compass is not emotionless apathy, but a state of calmness and serenity about your life that will naturally arise when you are on a mature, stable level of dealing with your experiences and emotions. .

It's important to note that the situation itself just happens. *It is what it is.* The subsequent emotional shifting on the compass is then based on *your interpretation* of the situation. This interpretation is quick and subconscious, based on *your values*.[2] This means that you

---

2. Branden (1972): The disowned self, p. 182ff

understand and modify the *calibration* of your emotional compass by looking at your values. There were several environments throughout my life where I was treated like a dog living with an alcoholic that has anger management problems - locked away, beaten or force-fed. And yet, a lot of the time, I didn't even mind. It just matched my calibration of how people can treat me, so there was little reason for anger to arise. I had to recalibrate my values around self-worth and respect entirely, before natural anger could spring up and fuel actions of self-defense.

Let's go back to the breakfast example. So if you had the value "*stealing from you is not ok*", then your breakfast being taken away might lead to anger. However, if you had the value "*my siblings can take whatever they like from me, because we are all family*", then your siblings taking your breakfast would lead to much less of an emotional response. As a consequence, that also means that your emotions can tell you about the values that you have but might not be aware of. Oftentimes, emotional reactions and patterns stem from long-term impacts connected to past experiences that have shaped our personality and that we have not fully resolved yet. If a woman I am dating doesn't want to kiss me, because perhaps she is busy eating an apple, the reasonable and mature emotional response would be to understand and accept this. However, if I have past experiences with parents or caregivers that made me feel like a burden or caused a wound for me, and that has not been resolved yet, I might be inclined to feel hurt and rejected. In this case, maybe I have hidden values and beliefs of "*I am a bothering burden*" that play into this. With some observation of the situation and my emotions, I can feel and observe that my emotions have their origins in a wound, and are not a mature, appropriate response to the situation. After all, I can just wait until she has finished eating her apple and then get the kiss I am looking for. This might seem like a ridiculous example to some readers, but this was actually the level of "*ermahgerd I'm so abandoned*" that I started dating with.

Understanding the purpose and value of all our potential emotions seems to be especially important in a culture that appears to be increasingly focused on the pursuit of constant happiness while blocking away any negative emotions. Emotions need to be acknowledged, experienced and expressed[3]. Even negative emotions have a healthy function. Resisting these emotions and locking them away can either lead to getting stuck with them, since they are never resolved, or with overall emotional apathy, by extending the emotion-blocking to all emotions[4]. I think that our overall goal in the context of emotions should be to let them flow instead of resisting them. Imagine if we pursued stable serenity instead of euphoric happiness, stemming from the ability to deal with our experiences. In my eyes, serenity has the potential to be lasting and to provide us with incredible depths of acceptance, gratitude and love.

So technically speaking, if any emotion comes up, we could be grateful for it. They either tell us stories about the world and our surroundings - like the need to set boundaries around safeguarding our breakfast. Or they tell us stories about our past, our wounds and the themes we have to work on if we want to improve our quality of life. Think of them *arising in you, like clouds and lightning arise in the sky*. Imagine if our first response upon any emotion entering our mind was gratitude. *Thank you for visiting me.* No matter if we are angry or hurt or joyful about things. Oh how much more we could then enjoy

---

3. Branden (1972): The Disowned Self, p. 33

4. Cf. Walker (2013): Complex PTSD p.38

the ups and downs of life! Rumi wonderfully captures this thought in his poem "the guest house":

The guest house

This being human is a guest house.
Every morning a new arrival.
A joy, a depression, a meanness,
some momentary awareness comes
as an unexpected visitor.
Welcome and entertain them all!
Even if they're a crowd of sorrows,
who violently sweep your house
empty of its furniture,
still, treat each guest honorably.
He may be clearing you out
for some new delight.
The dark thought, the shame, the malice,
meet them at the door laughing,
and invite them in.
Be grateful for whoever comes,
because each has been sent
as a guide from beyond.

Rumi

So, after being grateful for it visiting you, you could question if the emotion is situationally appropriate, or arising from an old wound that you might want to work on. Are you consciously aware of the value or belief that this emotion is based on? Do you accept this value as your own and not something that you accidentally inherited from your parents or society? Depending on your answers, the response can range from "acting the emotion out" to reflecting your emotions and listening to the stories they tell you about your past. Asserting my boundaries and telling my siblings not to steal my breakfast makes sense, right? While being angry at my partner or sulking or telling them off for not kissing me while eating an apple would feel rather silly, wouldn't it? In this case I could openly state my emotion, while communicating that I bear full responsibility and that it is upon me to remind myself that I am not a burden. Usually, just accepting and openly communicating these feelings will help a great deal to feel calm and mature again.

In the following sections, we will learn about deeply engraved, long-term emotional shifts. Once we can properly understand where emotions are coming from, we can learn in more detail about how to deal with them.

Chapter Three

Bonding and Trauma I

I'm in Colorado. Chasing after some Instagrammable late nine-teenth century wooden hut, built on the edge of a wild river. It's a mild midsummer afternoon. I'm also being chased by my girlfriend who is throwing stones at me. She would later say that she purposely missed, but it didn't even make a difference. The humiliation was much worse, anyways. Having to run from the person I love most in the world, because she is trying to physically hurt me. There she was, limping after me, in her grey dress. 'Dress' is a fancy word for the washed out piece of cloth going down to her knees. 'Tent' is what she actually called it. When she wore it, she was usually con-tent[1] as she liked to joke with a silly grin coming straight from the heart. Right now she wasn't very content. She was also obviously in immense pain and barely able to walk. Yet she was willing to bear the pain just to come after me - that's how committed she

---

1. Con is spanish for "with"

was to her anger. The road was going all the way around this one patch of land, so we ran - or limped in her case - in full circles, getting nowhere at all. It was bizarre. Once things calmed down, she took responsibility for what had happened, excused herself and stated that - after what she had done to me - we had to break up. No one can possibly remain in a relationship after being treated this way, right? Ha. Nope. I stayed. It was the same issue as my studies. How big would the dragon have to get, until I started looking at it? But this time it was deeper. This wasn't just about getting up in the morning and doing something with my time that could be remotely perceived as useful or meaningful. This time it went down to the core of who I am as a human being.

Why am I in this situation? Why am I not leaving? And what am I contributing to the situation? Life runs in patterns and important events are rarely a one-time thing. If it happened once, it will happen again. And it did happen again. We never managed to resolve conflicts in an ongoing manner. So any suppressed conflicts accumulated over several weeks until they finally erupted like a volcano. So every few weeks we would have conflicts entirely getting out of hand in a similar manner. And I still wouldn't leave. Also, partnerships - or any interactions - are never really one sided. It was tempting to blame her, but that just wouldn't do the trick. Up until that point in my life, she was the most lovable human being I had met. And I bear full responsibility for what is going on in my life. But why was *this* going on? In my eyes, I was just a friendly guy, mostly in control of his life and his emotions trying to have a stable relationship. But somehow I ended up in Colorado, having to run away from my partner. Turns out there were plenty of reasons for this happening; it was the natural consequence of who I was.

Humans have four basic psychological needs: attachment, autonomy, self-worth and pleasure. In early childhood, one is defenselessly dependent on one's environment to fulfill these needs. Unfortunately, two of them also contradict each other: the need for bonding and social connection is directly opposed to the need for autonomous decisions and having power over your own life - the so-called attachment-autonomy conflict. This means that even in the best and most loving environments, these basic needs are "violated" to some extent. It is impossible to always be parenting in the perfect "middle" between these two needs. Any affection towards a child will bear the opportunity cost of restricting its autonomy and any space given to the child bears the risk of not giving them sufficient attention. As long as a kid receives reasonable amounts of both love *and* autonomy in relation to their age and maturity, I don't see a problem with slight tendencies in one or the other direction.

Microtraumas

In this section and throughout the book, I am using the term "microtrauma" to differentiate between medical and psychological effects from a large, forceful impact, like a car crash, sexual abuse, or going to war (trauma) and subtle, slight behavioral impacts, that pretty much everyone experiences while growing up (microtrauma). This is obviously a stark simplification for the sake of illustration and in no way a comparison of different sufferings.

Humans are masters of adaptation to the surroundings they find themselves in. A metastudy indicated that people with spinal cord injuries were shown to have the same mental health, well-being and vitality as the general population in all studies where this score was computed[2]. I think this is both incredible and admirable. I don't find it appropriate to compare any sufferings, even though we might be tempted to think that "*others have it so much worse*" so we "*don't deserve to have problems ourselves*". I think that we are always entitled to strive for a higher quality of life and to find the problems we deal with to be challenging and demanding.

So. Microtraumas. Subtle, slight behavioural impacts that pretty much everyone can experience while growing up.

They can happen due to the patterns in the attachment behavior of caregivers, as well as with individual situations (e.g., a needle at the doctor's office violating a child's need for autonomy). In response to these injuries or microtraumas, the young person - a master of adaptation - develops a protective reaction. This makes evolutionary sense: If your siblings are eaten by bears, a fear of bears might help you survive. But in today's developed world it brings more disadvantages than advantages. Oftentimes, the original dangerous situation has long since passed but the protective reaction persists. What this protective response looks like depends on the age of the child, as well as the individual's conditioning to deal with trauma. An old colleague of mine developed a strong fear of balloons after one burst in front of her face in childhood and got caught in her eye. Protective reactions in bonding behavior are similarly logical: To a parent who does not give the child enough space, the child might react with closedness or withdrawal. This will enable the child to have sufficient autonomy, even in the environment of smothering parents. To an environment with great physical and psychological abuse, the child could react with a dissociative disorder - that is, the loss of the sense of self and the loss of reference to one's own body. This will prevent the child from having

---

2. Post, Noreau (2005): Quality of Life after Spinal Cord Injury

to physically feel the abuse suffered. Two things are important to note here. Firstly, this is not about being sick or healthy. In this context, a dissociative disorder, for example, is a learned protective reaction that is essential for survival and not a disease. Secondly, everyone, and I mean *everyone*, has had challenging experiences and developed behavioral and attachment patterns from them. Again, it is not a question of being sick or healthy, but only of in which direction and to what extent these patterns are present.

Protective patterns that are present to a very large extent are commonly captured in different psychological diagnoses, like ADHD, bipolar or borderline personality syndrome. In most cases, these behavioral patterns are just *healthy*, protective reactions to the environments that these people grew up in, but no longer live in.

I have never met a feeling or behaviour that did not make sense when viewed through the lenses of transference and traumatology

Pete Walker

Now, as adults, it is about healing and integrating these experiences to become a mature, stable person. The strong protective reactions are no longer necessary, but rather harmful to one's quality of life. Bessel van der Kolk, one of the leading scientists in trauma research, summarizes these different reactions and patterns in his diagnosis of *developmental trauma disorder*. It is a diagnosis that is supposed to capture individuals who were exposed to multiple traumas in childhood frequently, but don't match any of the existing diagnoses like PTSD, Autistic Spectrum Disorder (ASD) or Conduct Disorder. For me, this shows that it's not about pigeonholing people into different labels or sicknesses. It's about listening to a story, understanding the impacts of the story and processing connected experiences.It makes a lot of sense for a child that is physically or emotionally neglected to become very loud, needy and attention seeking in order to get the nurturing it needs. For a smothered and sheltered adolescent to fear suffocation and seek intensity to reach adequate levels of autonomy also seems reasonable.

Here is a small table showing in which direction these protective reactions can go at the behavioral level[3] . Note that young children tend to directly implement what they have been taught, while adolescents tend to lose themselves in the opposite:

Anxious (emotionally childish)	Avoidant (emotionally adolescent)	Secure (emotionally mature)
Feels useless	Feels perfect	Realistic, stable self-image
Overly emotional	Suppressing emotions	Authentic expression of emotions
Overly needy	Needless	Communicates Needs
Insecure	Defensive	Apologises when appropriate
Impulsive	Overly controlling	Flexible
Fears being alone	Fears being suffocated	Ok with both solitude and intimacy
Wants more intimacy	Looks for distractions	Healthy balance of needs
Idealises relationships	Disappointed by relationships	In reality about relationships

So how did all of this lead me to Colorado? To begin to understand, we have to go all the way back to 1996 when my father died of a brain tumor. I was two years old at the time. Understandably, my mother was slightly overwhelmed. After losing a partner of 25 years, it can be quite challenging to raise three children and rebuild a life that had originally been structured on the privilege of a lawyer's income while - most importantly - being a human being. She's a post-war era child, where gratitude for having food and a focus on keeping your shit together is much more important than doing fancy stuff like listening to your feelings.

So I spent the better part of my childhood and youth sleeping over at friends' places, staying in boarding schools or living overseas. I felt like a burden. Neither my parents nor "the system" seemed to have the capacity to deal with me. I felt like an ostrich. It's a bird, so it's supposed to be able to fly, right? But it can't fly, as it's too heavy. Too much of a burden. It cannot even hop a 1.8m fence to be a free, adult bird-citizen. Looking at the table above, there are several behaviors that can be used to describe my state back then.

- ***fears abandonment***: *my father died when I was two years old. Wicked tongues would say he abandoned me. At the age of two one cannot understand cause and effect. A two year old is likely to think that it is somehow at fault for the father "leaving". Being put into boarding schools surely feels like being abandoned. The fear of abandonment creates a constant need for reassurance that can be quite demanding for caretakers or partners.*

- ***seeks attention***: *seeking attention is a reasonable defense strategy for environments where attention to a child, its safety and its needs is scarce, isnt it? In my case, it led to being slightly louder and more emotional than "appropriate" in all sorts of situations.*

- ***idealises caretakers/partners***: *In half-orphans, the remaining caretaker usually creates a perfect mirror image of the lost partner. "If dad was still here, we wouldn't have these problems" I hear my mother say. Also, being able to stay afloat as a widow with three children and a job is somewhat heroic. I never really got to see her faults. I never really got to learn that it's perfectly natural for caretakers, partners, or people in general to be flawed and to not be perfect. Subsequently, I didn't see any flaws in (potential) partners.*

Another one that would fit quite well into this list is: **cannot stand an atmosphere of conflict**: *I could not stand any disharmony. I had to clear things up right away. I could not fall asleep during an argument.*

I poked at my partner long enough for her to talk to me and solve things, disrespecting any boundaries of hers in the process.

Idealizing potential partners prevented me from setting boundaries properly. "If dad was still here, we wouldn't have these problems" lead me to "if I had a partner, everything would be better". And if your partner is picture perfect, why would you need to set boundaries towards them? Being attention seeking, requiring reassurance and having to solve conflicts immediately can all lead to being a very demanding and exhausting partner. As I was not able to withstand a conflict and just go to sleep or put things aside for a while and then solve them later, it would lead to conflicts escalating unnecessarily throughout the relationship. All of this might begin to explain why I started the relationship, but it only scratches at the surface of things and it still doesn't explain why I remained in the situation. Why I tolerated having stones thrown at me. Why I didn't draw any lines for how I should be treated. My fear of being alone after a possible end to the relationship as well as my stubbornness (if this relationship doesn't work, I am going to make it work) aren't sufficient reasons. Why did I not leave?

Beliefs

The table of behaviors above is also closely connected to the second point: beliefs. It is actually a similar process to protective reactions, only described and illustrated differently. For an understanding of what I want to convey, I think it is important to read about both protective reactions as well as beliefs. In psychology, the following ideas reverberate with the concept of *"the inner child"*, first attributed to C. Jung. Stefanie Stahl has published marvelous and easy-to-read work in this direction with "The Child in You: The Breakthrough Method for Bringing Out Your Authentic Self". Basically, the inner child refers to the subconscious part of your personality. It is the origin of your emotions. In contrast stands the mature, grownup version of you, that can regulate these emotions and make conscious decisions on how you are going to deal with them. What kind of emotions originate from your inner child depends on the subconscious belief system that is connected to your inner child.

In the course of interacting with caregivers and others, the (actual) child is taught beliefs. Depending on the stage of developments that you can see in the table, these can be directly adopted or reversed. Beliefs create a mostly subconscious understanding of how the world works, what you are capable of and how you deserve to be treated in life. They are fundamental to our experiences and have a large influence on what we experience and how we deal with these experiences. Classic beliefs could be:

- I am not worth anything

- I am not welcome

- I am a failure

- I do everything wrong

- my self-worth depends on my academic performance

(all negative)

- I am loved

- I am allowed to make mistakes

- I am allowed to be a burden sometimes

- I am allowed to set boundaries

(all positive)

The connection between beliefs and protective reactions can be seen in sentences like "I have to do everything right", "I must not show any weakness" or similar. On one hand, *"I must not show weakness"* is a belief that might have been taught to the child at a young age. Men are often taught that they are not supposed to show emotions and that doing so is a sign of weakness. On the other hand, *"I must not show weakness"* is a protective reaction as the child might have been bullied by its peers for doing so.

Basically, we learn how to treat ourselves from our caregivers and our environment. We keep on treating ourselves like this long after we have moved out from home. Negative beliefs show themselves in adult life as criticism or shame, for example in the form of perfectionism, guilt, workaholism, catastrophizing or name-calling. For an improvement in quality of life, it is important to work on these negative beliefs. This is achieved by establishing positive beliefs, thought-stopping and substitution as well as inner "reparenting". Reparenting refers to developing the compassion for ourselves that we all deserve instead of the shaming and criticizing described above. We will discuss all of this in more detail in Part II.

Trauma

Everyone has these beliefs of how things work. Unfortunately, negative beliefs and protective reactions often go unnoticed in behavioural patterns in adult life and therefore cause problems. Trauma research can help us to understand why this is the case. So now to the third theoretical part and further explanation for microtrauma.

To explain the dynamics of trauma (Greek: τραύμα „wound, injury"), I will use a real life example - a car accident. However, the principles are just as useful for all the processes already described. When one experiences something ordinary, for example a visit to a theme park, this experience is processed and classified in the time afterwards. Afterwards, the memories coherently begin to blur and lose more and more detail, reality and depth. Think about a concert that you visited a few years back. Can you remember the smell of the room? Or the color of the other guests' outfits? Probably not. However, if a situation overwhelms or traumatizes you and the experience is not processed or classified, it remains present. Subsequently, it does not fade into a blurred, coherent memory, but remains in fragments in the mind of the traumatised person.

Back in 1999, Stan and Ute Lawrence were on their way from London, Ontario to Detroit for a business meeting[4]. They found themselves in sudden fog on the highway and got into the worst car crash in Canadian history. A total of 87 cars were involved. Stan and Ute had to watch helplessly while a girl burned in her car. They were trapped and could not free themselves. The perception of threat triggers an acute physiological response to prepare the body for just that. For the appropriate fight-or- flight response, there is an increase in oxygen support for the heart, lungs and throat. Digestive activities slow down or are interrupted. Facial muscles tense up and stress hormones are released. Trapped in a car, they were not able to implement a *fight-*

---

4. Lawrence (2009): The power of trauma, conquering post traumatic stress disorder

or-flight response - two common responses to dangerous situations[5]
. They experienced utter helplessness. A trucker ended up smashing their windshield with a fire extinguisher, freeing them in the process.

In the aftermath, Stan and Ute couldn't let go of what they had witnessed. They felt like they would die as soon as they relaxed or fell asleep. They were haunted by fragments of the unprocessed experience, whether at work, in the evenings or when they were trying to fall asleep. They were unable to forget the smell of leaking petrol, the view from the broken windscreen, the sound of cars shattering all around them.

Experiences that are not processed and classified remain present in the memory as well as the body. The body will keep the fight-or-flight response intact. It will release stress hormones because it thinks that the danger is still acute and current - a permanent state of stress and emergency that the body is not made for. It will also affect behavior and emotions - fear of cars, roads or any things that are in any way related to the car accident. One will systematically overestimate dangers related to cars. Since the threatening situation is considered to be "present" until the experience is resolved, the mind will keep perceiving reality in a distorted way. Any experience made will be "filtered" by the trauma perspective. As long as the body acts like it is still trapped in the dangerous situation, subconsciousness and behavior will act accordingly.

---

5. Freeze or Fawn are the two other danger-responses. For freeze, think of your response when hearing a sudden noise in the dark. For fawn, think of situations where you keep quiet to avoid starting a fight. The 4 F (fight, flight, freeze, fawn) can be used for classifying trauma-based behavioural patterns.

*Being traumatized means organizing your life from
now on, as if the trauma would still be happening -
unchanged and unchangeable - because every new event
is contaminated by the past.*

Bessel van der Kolk

Birth is a significant change in environment for us. We leave the protective, warm womb that comes with automated feeding and are instead born into a scary, bright and loud world. To cope with this helplessness, we are reliant on others for nurturing, protecting and surviving in general. Eye contact and physical touch are incredibly important at this age. It is no surprise that a lot of babies have a hard time dealing with separation from the mother at a very young age. Freud called this healthy narcissistic phase "his majesty the baby". Being separated from the mother implies being unprotected and in danger. The physiological response that comes with the perception of threat makes perfect sense in this case: a lot of babies will shout for their mother to come back to revert their attention back to the baby and end the separation; an infant will be stressed and on high alert until they are reunited with their mother.

American orphanages experienced staggering mortality rates between 90% and 100% in the early 20th century. This led to the spreading of foster care, where infants would receive more of the physical touch and emotional care they needed[6] . Higher physical affection in

---

6. Chapin, 1915, quoted in Montagu, 1971: Touching, the human significance of the skin

infants is also associated with lower levels of adult aggression[7] and secure attachment styles[8]. Now think of parents that are emotionally or financially incapable or even unwilling to fully tend to the child's needs. The baby will remain in this state of stress response for longer periods of time or even indefinitely. This feeling of fear, danger and abandonment will manifest itself as trauma until it is healed or re- solved. So even adult life might be led "...*as if the trauma would still be happening - unchanged and unchangeable - because every new event is contaminated by the past*".

It lies in the nature of trauma to be unbearable. A survivor just wants to forget and no longer be faced with what happened. Some people cannot even remember the terror that they have witnessed; their mind has blocked the memory as it would be too overwhelming to face. Meanwhile, the effects are still present in the subconscious, body and beliefs. Sexual abuse survivors could have trouble leading stable relationships, considering the other gender to be potential ag- gressors; veterans suffering from PTSD might lose themselves in alco- hol to drown out the memories, the pain or the guilt. The connection between having problems in today's life and a past trauma might not always be obvious or straightforward. However, it is not important to know every detail of what happened back then. It's more important to learn to deal with what you feel, what you do and what you think. To align body, mind and emotions and let what you come across flow freely. This will help you in letting the fragmented, present trauma evolve into a coherent experience that happened in the past. And

---

7. Prescott, 1971: Sensory deprivation vs sensory stimulation dur- ing early development

8. Anisfeld et al., 1990: Does infant carrying promote attachment?

even if a restructuring of beliefs might take much longer, initially recognizing irrational thoughts and behaviors can be a helpful start.[9]

The dynamic of trauma described above - to still be present and to be a filter that is applied to any objective reality - can be applied to the topic of microtraumas discussed earlier. For example, with basic needs that are not perfectly served: if we are criticized for everything in childhood, as adults we will hear criticism everywhere, even if none was expressed. Humans have a habit of shaping their environment according to their inner beliefs. If we feel worthless, we will notice negative gestures and facial expressions more than positive ones.[10] We will also surround ourselves with people who confirm and reinforce that feeling. Similarly, we tend to look for situations that match our traumatic experiences. Freud called these reenactments "repetition compulsion".[11] He liked to believe that a renewed confrontation with the trauma in reality holds the chance of perhaps processing, classifying and healing it this time. Unfortunately, there is little scientific basis for this thought as the repetition of traumatic experiences will more likely increase the suffering and re-traumatize the survivor, instead of solving it.

I personally think we are subconsciously looking for situations or surroundings that match our experiences and our trauma simply because it feels more *real*. It coincides with our beliefs and our inner landscape of the world and ourselves. If our experiences are aligned with our filter, then the filter doesn't distort the perceived reality anymore. For the first time, we have an almost objective view of reality.

---

9. Van der Kolk (2014): The Body keeps the Score, p. 144

10. Robson, 2022: The expectation effect, p.15ff

11. Freud, 1920: Beyond the Pleasure Principle

And reality itself, past all the filters, trauma and emotions, can be incredibly interesting.

So the goal in the context of trauma is to coherently process the past in a way where it stops "contaminating" the present and is merely a fading memory. It is to realize that whatever happened is part of the past. It is to feel adequately safe in your surroundings and to live in the present without applying a filter. The present is the only timespan that is real; only here can you do things, change circumstances or enjoy life. The past as well as the future are mere concepts in your head. It is not by chance that Eckhart Tolle has sold several million copies of "The Power of Now" going into the benefits of living in the present moment. So it seems quite reasonable to apply this concept not only to obviously traumatic experiences, but also to the subtle and hidden microtraumas and negative beliefs that we adopted in our childhood and that distort the way we perceive reality.

Ideally, we will reach a state of complete trust. On the one hand trust in ourselves: that we have sufficient capabilities to succeed in life as well as sufficient qualities to be accepted and loved as part of a community. On the other hand, trust in the universe: that we are completely safe, that we deserve good things to happen to us and that the flow of life is generally benevolent.

It's been one and a half years since Colorado. I am sitting on the carpet floor in the cozy room of my therapist. It's furnished like a living room, with armchairs, plants and a large, open bookshelf. That's right, I'm doing therapy now. I even talked to some of my friends about therapy. I

learned that it's okay to ask for help. It's okay to have emotions. It's okay to have problems. Admitting this actually shows strength, not weakness. That's what I am telling myself at least. It took me a long time to get past the stigma: "Men are not supposed to have emotions, are they? Me, in therapy? I'm not even sick! What am I supposed to do there?" But the dragon in my life was finally big enough - I knew I had to do something about it.

My personal self-development assistant is what I called her. She was incredibly calm, warm-hearted and created a safe space to work on myself. She provided me with her undivided attention. Oh, how lovely that was. She was also never afraid to ask the difficult questions or to tell me about my blind spots. I had plenty of them. I want to take you into one of my sessions back then in which I worked on discovering these blind spots:

I am doing the - here shortened - version of an exercise to discover my inner shadow child from Stefanie Stahl's book about the inner child. This exercise is supposed to help me identify my negative beliefs by looking at my environment as a child.

1. Picture one situation with your mom as a child that you thought was stupid.

   Oh that one is easy. I asked something of her. Affection, attention, recognition, whatever it was - her response would be: Not right now. I can't right now. While slightly raising her voice, as if she was annoyed by my existence and my needs.

2. Collect keywords. How was she?

   Busy. Stressed. Not affectionate. Not present.

3. Did you have a certain role or task in your family?

*Phew. Difficult. To stop existing? To stop getting on peoples'
nerves? Also to go down a cliché academic career path: excellent
grades, university and a job that is well paid, reputable and
requires a degree.*

4. Think of typical sentences that highlight your place.

"You little tyrant. You will do what I tell you".

5. Listen to your inner shadow child and think of the negative
   beliefs that you hold and that are the outcome of this environment

*I lived in several different environments over the course of
my childhood so I want to broaden this part of the exercise. I
want to put myself in the mental state I had as a child and
remember negative events that might have had an impact on
me.*

*I feel like I am a burden to my caregivers. I am exhausting. I am a
problem. I have no legitimacy to exist. I am an ostrich - I should be able
to fly, but I can't because I am too heavy and too demanding. I have to be
shoved off to my schoolmates' parents with trickery and manipulation.
I have to be sedated with pills and deported off to boarding school. I
feel my need for autonomy shaken to my core and violated and ignored
because I am being medicated without my knowledge and against my
will. I am in a boarding school for which I do not have the necessary social
skills. I am being bullied and excluded by students as well as teachers. I*

don't know how to set boundaries; I also don't know how to respect the boundaries of others.

I am being beaten and locked away, while my caregivers don't take appropriate measures to ensure my safety. I am forced by my caregivers against my explicit will to eat foods that I find repulsive. Why is my fate in their hands? At least the problem is solved and no longer shouts and screams and bothers.

What are the exact negative beliefs resulting from these experiences? I feel like "*I deserve to be treated badly*" summarizes it well, no matter what the exact abuse would look like.

Chapter Four

Bonding and Trauma II

Bonding and relationships

As a quick summary of the last chapter: we all apply a filter to reality, based on the experiences or traumas that we have not fully dealt with yet. Microtraumas can cause subtle filters and emotional responses in a similar fashion. Beliefs serve as a concept that illustrates all of this; we believe in what we are told as a child. We learn our self-worth as well as how benevolent the world is to us as children. This subconsciously influences our personalities, behaviour and our view of the world.

Before I make any further reference to our behavior and our patterns, I would like to clarify a few things. You and I, at our core, are kind and loving and deserving of love. When I speak critically (analyzing) aspects of our behavior here, it is about the relationship between us and other people and not about you or me as a human being. These aspects were essential for us to survive in the past in order to cope with the things we experienced and therefore have a full right to exist.

We encounter these patterns in everyday life, with friends, in our careers, at school or university. Whenever there is a situation that resembles patterns of where we have been hurt, we are inclined to act out of the wound, not out of a mature stable place. Maybe we strongly react to criticism or we have trouble with big decisions or we avoid conflicts at all costs.

These kinds of feelings tend to take control of our actions quickly and strongly. It feels different when they do. If we could recognize when we are acting out of this wound, we could much better experience and regulate our emotions.

These patterns also create the foundations of our relationships. We look for partners that treat us the way we learned to be treated and that treat us the way we think we should be treated.

We accept the love we think we deserve

Stephen Chbosky in "The Perks of Being a Wall-flower"

Generally, there are different ways we deal with trauma - thinking back to the table of behaviors in the Microtrauma section. So for example, for some people, nothing feels *real* anymore, unless they reenact the trauma and stay in harmful relationships, or unless they do something extreme like parachuting. Or my personal, old strategy was to block the trauma out as much as possible, e.g. by playing computer games or drinking or just distracting myself in general. Overall, there are many different possible responses to our wounds. This is just a framework for approximation.

In relationships, however, there are usually two directions this can go into: the anxious and the avoidant attachment style. The behaviors of these roles correlate with the table in the section about Microtraumas. The anxious person idealizes caretakers or partners, while the avoidant person is disappointed and feels suffocated by caretakers or partners. We can have elements of both or play different roles in different situations; though generally people tend to lean more towards one or the other.

> *"When an avoidant and an anxious person begin a relationship, a predictable pattern occurs: the avoidant gives and gives, sacrificing his own needs, but it's never enough for the anxious one. So the avoidant grows resentful and seeks an outlet outside of the relationship, but at the same time feels too guilty to stop taking care of the needy person."*

Lorraine in "The Truth"[1]

In most relationships, one can observe these patterns at least to a certain degree. The avoidant goes above and beyond their own capac-

---

1. Quote slightly adapted to fit the wording used here. Quote from Neil Strauss (2015): The Truth: An Uncomfortable Book About Relationships

ity of caring and tending to the needs of the anxious one. However, the anxious person always wants more. These needs can relate to anything around intimacy - sex, physical touch and spending time together are the most common ones. The avoidant - that is already giving more than they really want to - blames the anxious that it's never enough. It results in resentment towards the partner, in feeling suffocated by the relationship and in looking for distraction outside of the relationship. This distraction can be in obvious forms like flirting or cheating with other people. It can also appear in less obvious forms like becoming a workaholic, doing extreme sports, taking stimulants or just really doing any activity excessively to avoid intimacy with the partner. The anxious one in turn can feel that the partner is starting to move away or avoid intimacy. They can experience *real* abandonment, on top of the imagined abandonment that they felt at the beginning of the relationship or before. Therefore, they require even more reassurance and tend to put even more pressure on the partner to receive the desired level of intimacy. The anxious one also looks for blockers that make the pain go away, like numbing drugs, computer games or similar.

And then, either by an undeniable incident, or just by the continuous decline of the relationship, the anxious one reaches the awareness that ends the fantasy of their idealized partner. Colorado was certainly an undeniable incident for me. And then the cycle starts from the beginning, either with the same partner or in a different relationship.

Imagine things happening on a spectrum:

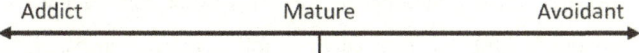

Addict   Mature   Avoidant

An addict that is very far out on the spectrum might (falsely) imagine their partner to be the love of their life and be ready to marry them, while not realizing that their partner - an avoidant very far on the right of this spectrum - might have already decided to end the relationship.

I don't think that the goal is to be perfect or to avoid any patterns altogether. Instead, I think the goal is to reach an understanding of what is going on, to realize when you are feeling needy (in line with the anxious attachment style) or resentful (like an avoidant) and to be *somewhere* around the middle. To be *good enough*. But what does it mean to be in the middle of this spectrum or to be "mature"?

It could mean to not be constantly caught up in the relationship dynamic, but to treat the relationship as a third entity. Something that can be nurtured together, while both partners are also freely able to transition back into a state of individuality and freedom, without being dependent on the partner's attention and without having to flee from the partner's pressure.

This is called an interdependent relationship. Basically, you are constantly transitioning back and forth between a state of companionship and a state of individuality. For this to work, you need to have a life outside of your partner to come back to. This can include hobbies, friends, projects or activities. Anything that gives you fulfillment and satisfies your needs. If you spend 24/7 with your partner, while never transitioning back to being alone and independent, conflict is bound to happen. As nice and as powerful as it might feel - you are still different human beings, with differences in preferences, opinions or way of life. These differences will come out sooner or later and will result in conflict if you are not able to give or take the necessary space to express them. An avoidant is usually not able to take the space that they require while secretly blaming the partner for that. Someone with an anxious attachment style is usually not able to grant their partner the space that they need, out of fear of abandonment. Once again, think of a spectrum, this time displaying the level of intimacy:

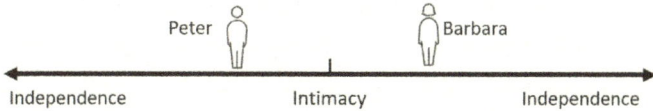

In the middle, around intimacy, would be spending time together, living together, being affectionate, being honest and open about what is going on. Let's imagine the person on the right, Barbara, is moving towards independence. For example, in the form of a message saying: "Hey, I need a couple of days for myself, I will come back to you". Or alternatively, in the form of not responding to messages or making less time for the relationship and their partner.

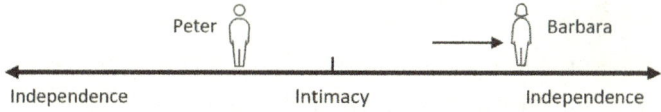

What would an anxious response look like? He or she would likely feel abandoned. There might be little structure or fulfillment outside of the relationship. There might be fear of abandonment and a feeling of neediness as well as a demand for reassurance. One might question the partner's action, might need an explanation or justification or might even be jealous and question the loyalty of Barbara. On the scale of intimacy and independence, a response would probably look like this:

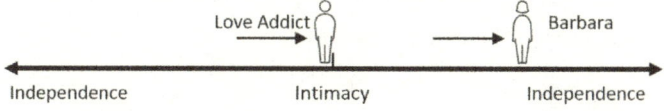

The move towards intimacy would try to re-establish the level of intimacy that they had together before Barbara needed space. This move would include increased "investment" to make up for the lack of investment on Barbara's side. This could be "achieved" by initiating more conversations in writing, calling, and trying to initiate plans together. All of this would ignore Barbara's need for space. Reestablishing the old level of distance while having an obvious imbalance in the level of investment into the relationship would create a feeling of suffocation for Barbara. Barbara then has to move away even further to find the desired space for herself.

This turn of events could also happen in reverse order. The anxious person approaches Barbara to initiate more intimacy or to receive more reassurance. Barbara then moves away to create the old level of distance which, in turn, makes the feeling of abandonment and the need for reassurance even worse for the anxious person. Real abandonment doesn't even have to take place for someone with an anxious attachment style to feel abandoned. They would naturally be more inclined to notice negative behavior or action towards them. They would interpret abandonment even when there isn't any. We don't see things as they are, we see things as *we* are.

So, what would a healthy and mature response from Peter look like when Barbara is moving away? He would move an equal amount of distance to the left towards independence to mirror Barbara's actions. In the given example, he could respect her wish for a couple of days to herself and just be like "Sure, just hit me up once you are ready to talk again" and then go silent, granting his partner with the space she has asked for. He could also signal acceptance and support with words like "No worries - I am here if you need me".

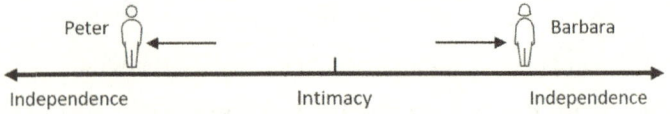

Barbara would feel respected and seen, and she would get the space she asked for. After a few days or whenever she feels ready, Barbara can re-initiate intimacy, make plans with Peter and go back towards intimacy.

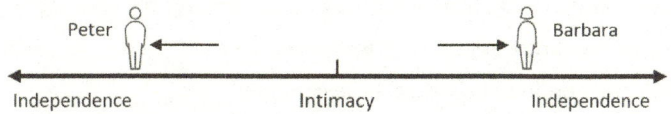

This dynamic is applicable on the micro- as well as on the macro level. So in everyday situations while hanging out, Barbara might want to reduce the cuddling or be alone for a few minutes or keep a topic to herself. The best thing Peter can do is to respect that, to wait for Barbara to come back, or to approach her again after a reasonable amount of time has passed, while respecting that she might still need more space. On a macro level, Barbara might want to spend a day or two alone, or she might even want to stop talking to Peter for a while or might not want to see him for some time. Running after her or putting pressure on her to go back to talking would only make things worse. We can only ever experience as much intimacy as *both* partners want.

Above, we looked at Peter's possible response if he had an anxious attachment style. But what would Barbara's problems look like if she was an avoidant? She would remain in a level of intimacy that she is not comfortable with. She might not be comfortable with this level of intimacy because she is afraid of being hurt if she shows herself to be that vulnerable. Maybe she saw what happened to her parents' relationship and wants to avoid the same fate in her own life. She might remain in the situation possibly out of guilt and feeling responsible for her partner's perceived abandonment. In this scenario, she would need to learn that she is not responsible for Peter's feelings. We are not responsible for our partners' or our parents' or anyone else's feelings! If Peter doesn't like the level or type of intimacy that Barbara provides (or lack thereof), he is free to leave her. She would also feel suffocated because she doesn't authentically set the boundaries and create the space that she needs. She might then blame Peter for the suffocation, instead of taking responsibility for herself, communicating her needs and setting boundaries where she needs them.

So what do we do with this spectrum? Overall we want to move from a *needy -> resentment* dynamic towards a balanced dynamic, where both partners are able to transition back and forth between being independent and investing into the relationship. Anxious people need to learn to grant their partners the space that they might need. This goes hand in hand with learning to accept being alone without feeling abandoned. Avoidants need to learn to take the space that they might need. This is also helpful in becoming more comfortable with expressing feelings, showing vulnerability and being intimate with others.

If we develop our lives and our self-image outside of the relationship sufficiently, we can develop emotional outcome-independence. This means accepting the possibility of the relationship ending at any point in time, because you know that you will be okay, no matter what happens. This independence enables us to have difficult conversations, to openly communicate our needs and to respect our partners' choices. Anxious people also often have trouble setting boundaries because they are scared that their partner will leave as soon as they demand to be treated well. The knowledge that you have a stable life outside of the relationship will make anything that happens within the relationship much healthier and stronger since you are not dependent on any level of intimacy or any outcome.

Even if we can still feel and observe neediness or suffocation or resentment, we can already learn to observe what is going on inside of us, to accept this and to communicate these feelings openly. Saying

"*Hey, I feel slightly pressured, I feel like I need more time to myself*"
or "*Hey, somehow I am a little insecure, can we quickly discuss where
this might be coming from?*" is much better than just acting things
out. For conversations like these, it is extremely important to take full
responsibility for your own feelings and to not blame your partner
for them. No one can *make* you feel anything. You are responsible for
how you feel. You're not happy with what your partner is doing or
not doing? Well, surely you can ask them to change. But any change
should be seen as a bonus. For your own sake, you have to either accept
them the way they are, or leave. Not sleeping together as much as you
would like? You are free to find a partner that provides you with what
you need, but don't blame your partner if they are not providing in the
way you imagined. You can only be grateful for what they are willing
to compromise for the relationship. This goes both ways - you are also
not responsible for how your partner feels. You can't *make* them feel
anything. If they are not happy with what you are bringing into the
relationship, they are free to leave.

- learn to be alone and learn to give space (as an anxious person)

- learn to be intimate and learn to take space (as an avoidant)

- increase outcome independence

- communicate openly

- (learn to) set and respect boundaries

One more thing. I don't think relationships are the determining
factor for your quality of life. If I am miserable in a relationship, there
is a good chance I am miserable outside of the relationship, too. I think
that relationships are mere mirrors of our self-love and maturity. I

don't think there are any white knights or princesses out there coming to our rescue if we are miserable in the first place. Don't get me wrong, intimate relationships are wonderful and important. However I think that ultimately, healthy relationships will only feel real once we have a healthy relationship with ourselves and compassion for ourselves.

So. Colorado. Why was I in this situation? Why was I not leaving? And what was I contributing to the situation? In the meantime, I learned about microtraumas and being a wounded child. I feared abandonment, would seek attention and idealize partners. I could not stand an atmosphere of conflict. I also learned about trauma and beliefs. I felt like I deserved being treated badly, I felt like an alien that doesn't properly fit in. And I had a lot of unresolved trauma of being abandoned, beaten or forced to eat. I also learned about anxiousness, avoidance, and relationship patterns. But where do I personally fit into the neediness-resentment dynamic?

I obviously had an anxious attachment style. I entered the relationship to end the pain of abandonment and connected in a fog of fantasy of having found "the perfect partner". Any space she would want to take for herself I translated into a feeling of being rejected and abandoned. I ignored her need to have a life of her own. I was basically looking for dating experiences that mirrored my environment as a child and what I had been taught at a young age. In essence, she held up a big fat mirror saying: "This is who you are, Fred. This is what feels most real to you. This is the experience you are willing to deal with in order to have a relationship. This is what your image of yourself and the world looks like". She was very persistent in holding up this mirror to make me aware of my blind spots and I am extremely grateful for her to have done so. She could have left just as well and I gave her plenty of reasons to do so.

Oddly enough, her behavior resembles a concept applied in a therapy form called "provocative therapy"[2] that came to life in the sixties and seventies in the States. In it, the therapist externalizes the patient's darkest thoughts and beliefs and verbally mirrors them to them. This way, the patient is pushed to recognize how unfavorable their beliefs are. Patients are also nudged towards learning to assert themselves against these externalized thoughts and beliefs. Crucial for the success of this therapy form is the unconditional positive regard that the therapist has to radiate while verbally challenging the patient. And well, you might question if she radiated unconditional positive regard for me while throwing stones at me, but she certainly had it before and afterwards. So you could argue that she created an environment that was beneficial (and probably even necessary) for me to learn to set boundaries and assert myself since I had never learned how to do that as a kid. Indicators for this were that, on very rare occasions, I let a glimpse of aggression shimmer through in these sorts of incidents. And her reaction always seemed to be one of joy upon me finally showing some form of aggression, even if I merely used it to assert myself. I never fully understood her response in this regard but I like to believe that on some level she knew that aggression (or determined assertion) was the healthiest response I could have shown in these conflicts.

Ok, so apart from the belief of "this is how I am supposed to be treated" which plays well into the earlier mentioned phenomenon of repetition compulsion or trauma reenactment, and apart from a general fear of abandonment, there was also a fear of not finding someone who would

---

2. Farrelly, Brandsma (1974): Provocative Therapy

"hit the mark" as well as she did. Which is ironic and slightly funny. It felt "real" - the whole experience just matched my filter and let everything else blur in comparison.

So, as much gratitude as I have for her having been in my life - I don't think that this was about her specifically. I think it was just the experiences that felt real for me. If it wasn't her, I would have just met someone else one, two, three years before or after that and ended up with similar experiences. If I was alone, I would have felt alone and abandoned. If I was with her (or someone else), any interaction would have made me feel like a rejected burden, like an ostrich, no matter how healthy the person was or how much it was coming from the heart. As long as I didn't solve my filter, as long as I didn't realize that my traumatic experiences were all just a long-gone part of the past, my life would look like this.

So where did I go after Colorado? I went to do years of conversational gestalt therapy. I went to explore my negative beliefs; I went to think about how I want to be treated and how I can communicate the results to my environment. Until today, I have learned that I am responsible for my surroundings. I have learned to be aware of my needs and my body. To nourish myself with lovingly cooked food. To feel my appetite. To listen to my feelings. To understand if I am being rejected or just irrationally afraid of it. I have learned that I can express myself as I am, think and feel without fearing social repercussions. Ok to be honest, I have not fully learned that one yet - sometimes I pull cheeky jokes that keep me wondering for days if people are secretly pissed off or weirded out by them. Last week I jokingly turned a work meeting into a self-help group, told my colleague "Thank you for sharing" and started talking about the "existential dread that creeps up on all of us". That was fun. Anyways, I'm drifting off. I have also learned to respect other people's boundaries. I have learned that love towards me is a tender, voluntary *plant that only thrives if I give it space to flourish. I have learned that I have a right to exist and that I am not a burden to anyone. I have learned that my feelings serve important functions. My anger shows me when my boundaries are being crossed. My sadness helps me to process difficult experiences. I have learned that other people only have as much power over me as I give them. I have learned that no one has the privilege to treat me badly. My boundaries, where I set them, have a full right to exist and serve a purpose of protecting me as well as my mental and physical well-being. How did I get here? Part II will lay out the tools that helped me on my journey. I still use them today either regularly, or when I need to resolve emotions and experiences.*

The Self in Flow

Part II

Chapter Five

The Body keeps the Score

After observing a possible correlation between sexual abuse in childhood and severe obesity in adulthood in their patients, a group of scientists set out to take a closer look at the possible impacts of adverse childhood experiences (ACEs) on problems in adulthood[1]. The possible categories of adverse experiences included physical, sexual or emotional abuse, as well as neglect or witnessing of maternal battering[2]. The study aimed to explore possible correlations with

---

1. Felitti et al. (1998): Relationship of childhood abuse and household dysfunction to many of the leading causes of death in adults. The Adverse Childhood Experiences (ACE) Study

2. The Anna Institute: Finding your ACE Score. Online at: https://www.theannainstitute.org/Finding%20Your%20ACE%20Score.pdf

health problems in adulthood like alcoholism, drug abuse, depression, sexually transmitted diseases, or health-related quality of life. The results were astonishing, both in terms of how widespread ACEs were, as well as the clear connection of an increase in ACEs leading to an increase in health problems and social issues.

> *"The ACE Study findings suggest that certain experiences are major risk factors for the leading causes of illness and death as well as poor quality of life in the United States. It is critical to understand how some of the worst health and social problems in our nation can arise as a consequence of adverse childhood experiences. Realizing these connections is likely to improve efforts towards prevention and recovery."*

Centers for Disease Control (CDC)[3]

More than 60% of respondents had at least one type of ACE, 38% at least two different types, and almost one in six had experienced four or more different types of ACEs[4]. This includes things like

- *"often being sworn at, insulted, humiliated or put down"*,

- *" often feeling that no one in your family loved you or thought you were important"* or

---

3. Online at: https://nicic.gov/weblink/adverse-childhood-experiences-ace-study

4. CDC, online at: https://www.cdc.gov/violenceprevention/aces/fastfact.html

- *"having an adult or person at least 5 years older touch you or have you touch their body in a sexual way"*

Participants that experienced at least four different types of adverse experiences had...

- *4- to 12-fold increased health risks for alcoholism, drug abuse, depression, and suicide attempt;*

- *a 2- to 4-fold increase in smoking, poor self-rated health, > or = 50 sexual intercourse partners, and sexually transmitted disease; and*

- *1.4- to 1.6-fold increase in physical inactivity and severe obesity,*

while there was a *"graded relationship to the presence of adult diseases including ischemic heart disease, cancer, chronic lung disease, skeletal fractures, and liver disease"*[5].

Overall, it is more likely than not that a grown adult in today's society has had experiences in their childhood that were possibly traumatic, where their core needs weren't tended to, or which caused them to develop protective patterns that are still active today. Bear in mind that subtle protective patterns in the context of microtraumas, as discussed before, are likely to not even show up as an ACE. Therefore, I believe that everyone can benefit from understanding where they come from, as well as from being more empathetic towards the

---

5. Felitti et al. (1998): Relationship of childhood abuse and household dysfunction to many of the leading causes of death in adults. The Adverse Childhood Experiences (ACE) Study

struggles of others, and from improving their toolbox on dealing with life and its unavoidable ups and downs.

To be more bold - I don't think it's even necessary to argue in relationships (or anywhere else for that matter), but instead to always discuss things in a calm and reflective manner. As long as one of two partners is acting from a mature point of view at any given time, there is no need for arguments. Imagine a life where you just *don't* fight. Maybe some heated discussions with a few jokes in between. Maybe coming to conclusions that there are just differing opinions. Or maybe breaking body contact for a while. But no name calling, no aiming to cause emotional damage, no shouting. Never. It's us against the problem, not you against me. It is possible.

Noise. Blur. I'm in my kitchen. My partner is talking. What is she saying? I must've missed a sentence or two. Something's off. My gut is clenching and my chest is tightening. I don't want to keep listening, I want to run away and cry. Why? Did she say anything? Think. No time to think. I still have to listen. Something about university. I nod and wait for her to be done talking. I make use of the lull in the conversation and sneak off to my room. To bed. To safety. My blanket protects me from all evil. My thoughts are racing.

It wasn't very mature of me to sneak off. It's not like she's not going to notice. I just want to cry and deal with my feelings and then I'll go back. Did she say anything aggressive? Do I have to set some boundaries? It was just a conversation about... No, I think it was all just casual conversation. But something must have pushed my buttons. Ok Fred, I love you. And that girl in the kitchen loves you too. She ain't here to hurt you. And even if she was - she only ever has as much power as I give her, okay? You're safe. Protected. It's alright.

God, this inner child stuff talking to myself feels weird. But I also feel like it helps, like I'm parenting myself. I picture myself as a young child, that is the reason for me starting to dissociate and for my chest tightening. About ten minutes have passed until she comes barging in.

Wasn't this what I had hoped for? That she would follow attentively to hold and love me - You could've just told her to do that, you know - yeah but you don't tell people to love you, that's not how it works. Doesn't it show more reassurance when she has the idea by herself? - Now that's just silly, do you want reassurance or love? By this time I've realized that she hasn't exactly come in to love me and hold me. She is rather angry. "Why are you sneaking off and hiding in bed and pulling your shit again? Just talk to me so I know what's going on".

As long as at least one person is in the adult function at any given time, there is no need for an argument. Right. So, with the "just talk to me so I know what's going on"part, she is kind of right. And for the anger - I know what she's doing. She is taking responsibility for my sadness and for me being hurt. She feels like I blame her and give her the fault for not tiptoeing around my feelings like a good Disney princess. That's her "filter", hearing blame for other people's feelings where there is none.I don't blame her. I know that it's on me, how I feel. That's my "filter", feeling sad and abandoned by things coming up in casual conversation.

I'd had ten minutes to look at my feelings and to accept them. I also understand where she is coming from, which helps me to be a good grownup again. I explain to her that she did nothing wrong and that all is well. I also recognize that openly communicating my state in the kitchen would probably have been the more mature thing to do. "Hey, I'm feeling kind of sad right now, I'll need 15 minutes to myself and *then I'll be back" or "feel free to join me and console me, if you want to". Maybe next time I will have the maturity to do so. So, I ask her to give me five more minutes to get my shit together and then I'll be back in the kitchen for our dinner.*

All of us experience situations that are hard to accept or hard to deal with. The following part of the book should give you an overview of possible approaches, authors or ideas that, if they speak to you personally, you can go into more depth with. I consider it a toolbox to revert to if you are in difficult situations or if you recognize patterns in your life. A toolbox to resolve our internal resistance. It contains elements to implement in your life as a safety net for overwhelming emotions in the heat of the moment, and for overwhelming patterns that are generally manifesting in your life. I hope that it inspires activities and habits that will make you feel safe and powerful and that help you reach your potential and desired state of mind. As painful as it might be, emotional wounds are like gold for you to dig up and uncover. They tell you stories about how life works and about things that you can learn. Moreover, they make you unique as a person. Nobody else has had the exact same experiences as you, so learning from your experiences and sharing these insights can bring immense value to others and society in general.

Those who stick with a long term recovery process are often rewarded with emotional intelligence far beyond the norm

Pete Walker[6]

Of course, this only applies once these issues are solved and healed. Unresolved experiences can cause terrible suffering and make life extremely challenging and difficult.

Also, it seems societally shameful to repeatedly feel negative emotions or to deal with psychological healing. When I break my arm, I go to a physical doctor to heal. If I'm hurt in my emotional nature, I seek out a psychological doctor to help me heal. And that's okay and all good. It increases my quality of life immensely as it leads to loving myself, being well, and having more love for my fellow human beings.

Basically, it's just communicating to the body and the brain that the original stressful or dangerous situation is over and that you are

---

6. Walker (2013): Complex PTSD, p. 68

competent and worthy of love. Negative experiences cannot be un-done, but the disruptive emotional and physical reaction in our body is what we can learn to deal with. Once again, imagine a spectrum on which your arousal as your response to danger and trauma are put on one side, while safety, visceral connection as well as the capacity for playfulness and creativity are put on the other side.

Hyperarousal   Relaxation
   Trauma   Safety

Ideally, we want to have the tools and capacity to freely move along this spectrum in both directions. In the short term, moving towards a feeling of relaxation and safety can be helpful to not be overwhelmed by our emotions or memories. The long-term motivation towards relaxation is also rather clear - to completely resolve trauma, instead of just avoiding it in the moment. Sometimes, before we can start to deal with trauma, a general feeling of safety and relaxation has to be established in the first place. Moving in the other direction - to the left - implies a capacity to withstand and resolve states of hyperarousal. This way we can carefully confront uncomfortable situations and experiences with a confidence to not be (re-)traumatized, but to rather resolve the issue once and for all. Putting these steps into chronological order gives us the following chain of action:[7]

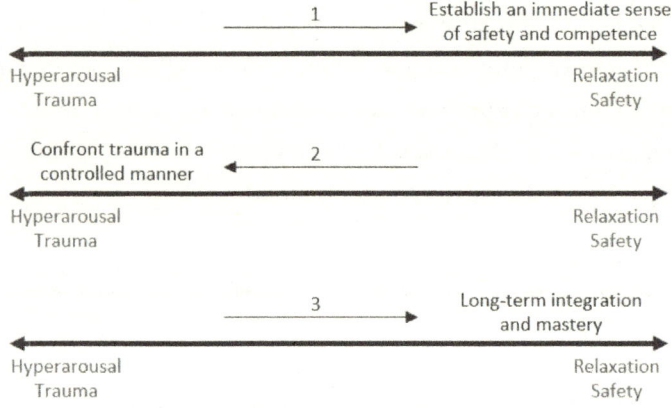

Most of the tools presented in this part of the book are in one way or another linked to one of these three steps or fill them with life. I want to look at trauma research and see which insights we can apply to microtraumas, to our subtle tendencies in bonding behaviour or to any other hurdles we may encounter. Ideally, we can use these ideas and tools for any challenging experiences we have in life, even if we don't have any adverse childhood experiences or any mental health problems to solve.

The body-mind highway is a two-way street

The nervous system connects your brain with your body. This means that your mood and emotions are reflected in your facial expressions and body posture. When you are sad, you might have hanging shoulders, an arched back and it might show on your face. Jordan Peterson wonderfully illustrates the connection between mood, facial expression and posture in the first chapter of his book "12 Rules for

Life"[8] . He uses research from lobsters to illustrate this. Lobsters are highly competitive and often fight for their place in lobster society. After winning fights and upon gaining higher status positions in their hierarchy, they will have "better" posture and higher levels of serotonin. Serotonin is believed to boost your mood, lead to higher confidence as well as regulate your posture; in lobsters as well as in humans. So this connection is fairly obvious. When we are in a great mood, we will radiate happiness on our face and we will stand up straight with our shoulders back and our chest out.

However, what is less known and less obvious: the tail can also wag the dog! This whole connection also works the other way around. We can greatly influence our mood by what we do with our faces, and (more importantly) what we do with our bodies. If you consciously move your facial muscles, one by one, into a position of a happy face, you will report feeling happier[9] . The vagus nerve connects the body with internal organs such as the heart, lungs and stomach. A stunning 80% of the fibers in this key nerve are directed *towards* the brain[10] . This means that we directly influence our brain, our arousal regulation and our mood by the way we move, the way we breath and by our posture. Isn't that incredible?

Think of step 1 above. "Establish an immediate sense of safety and competence". Whenever we are in a state of hyperarousal, where

---

8. Jordan Peterson (2018): 12 Rules for Life: An Antidote to Chaos, p.23ff

9. Kleinke, Peterson, Rutledge (1998): Effects of self-generated facial expressions on mood. Referenced in Peterson (2018).

10. Porges (2010): Stress and Parasympathetic Control. Referenced in Van der Kolk (2015)

emotions might be overwhelming us, we can start by taking a few very slow and deep breaths, in through the nose and out through the mouth, while paying attention to the breaths themselves. Some of the following tools will also make use of this connection. They will include moving the body and expressing yourself to establish a sense of safety and well-being.

The benefits of Yoga

So with these tools we have a few key aims and goals in mind:

- To be in the present moment

- To rid ourselves from the past and to not be stuck in it

- To learn to deal with disruptive emotional and physical reactions to trauma in our body

- To achieve a general feeling of safety and relaxation

- To have compassion for ourselves

- To increase consciousness and awareness of life

There is one thing that achieves *all* of that. Yoga. It encourages present-moment experience, listening to inner impulses, moving rhythmically and interacting positively with others[11] . Sudarshan Kriya Yoga, for example, has been shown to be an effective adjunct to the

11. Emerson, Hopper (2011): Overcoming Trauma through Yoga

treatment of issues like stress, anxiety, post-traumatic stress disorder (PTSD), depression, substance abuse and rehabilitation of criminal offenders.[12] The study in this context names proper training by a skilled teacher and a 30-minute practice every day as key factors to maximize the benefits.

Yoga turned out to be a terrific way to (re)gain a relationship with the interior world and with it a caring, loving, sensual relationship to the self

Bessel van der Kolk

Bessel van der Kolk has, together with colleagues, conducted similar research. It has shown that patients who failed to respond to any other medication or treatment had their PTSD symptoms markedly reduced by just ten weeks of yoga practice[13]. In his programs, a rather simple approach was used to help the patients; this included things like learning to notice and count in and out breaths, as well as learning to notice muscle activity in different postures.

Just a week-long yoga retreat was enough for me to observe benefits. However, after I further read about the scientific extent of the positive impact, I was still genuinely surprised. Yes, it is pretty much common knowledge that yoga aids well-being, but on this scale? Yoga usually

---

12. Brown, Gerberg (2005): Sudarshan Kriya Yogic breathing in the treatment of stress, anxiety, and depression: part II—clinical applications and guidelines

13. Van der Kolk, et al. (2014): Yoga As an Adjunctive Treatment for PTSD

combines meditation, moving the body (asanas) and breathing practices (pranayama)[14] . The more I read into it and connected that to my own experiences, the more it made sense. It tends to your spiritual needs with meditation; to your physical needs with holding postures that make good use of your muscles and it cares for emotional needs as you actively spend time with yourself. There is no distraction like the TV or your phone. It is just you and your observations of your mind, emotions and body. Being able to notice and interpret what we are feeling in our bodies is a key step to truly knowing ourselves. It can also be incredibly helpful and supportive in recovery to know how to stay relaxed and use calm breathing when we are approaching painful memories with the hopes of resolving them.

Exercising & going to the gym

When at an absolute low and feeling nothing but despair, confusion and helplessness, I find that practical advice can be more helpful than theorizing about concepts or the roots of your issues. It's sometimes not necessary to understand your problem to be able to fix it. If you don't know where to start, or what to do, there are two things that come to my mind:

- Clean your room

- Go to the gym

---

14. Overall, the term yoga can refer to plenty of other practices, too. Here I mostly refer to the modern, western way of it.

Tidying your room will be discussed later on, and about going to the gym: it just makes you feel good - simple as that! For me, exercising about three times a week feels like paying rent to my body - it allows me to use a body that is roughly in shape and capable of moving itself and other stuff around.

From a scientific perspective, exercise increases levels of endorphins, which are basically the brain's natural feel-good chemicals. It improves mood state and self-esteem as well as reducing stress and anxiety levels. Moreover, it's associated with feelings of mastery and self-efficacy and might also distract from (or even resolve) feelings of depression and anxiety.[15] Other benefits include enhanced cognitive function, a better sleep quality and - who would have thought - changes in your physical appearance.

Exposure to cold - a real life cheat code

Back in 2014, Germany beat Algeria in overtime at the World Cup knockout stages after a tough match. This was when I first heard about exposure to cold. In the legendary post-match interview, a beat-up Per Mertesacker, grumpy about the critical line of questioning said: "*I'm going to lie in a barrel of ice for three days, then we'll analyze the match and take it from there*". (One of his other responses was: "*Do you think there is a circus of clowns among the last 16 teams?*"). All I knew back

---

15. For a good overview, see Mikkelsen et al. (2017): "Exercise and mental health"

then was that athletes apparently benefit from cold water immersion in their recovery process after intense exercise.

It took another six years for me to stumble upon Wim Hof through a friend. Wim Hof, nicknamed "the Iceman", is known for doing fun things like climbing Mount Kilimanjaro in two days or running a marathon north of the polar circle - wearing only shorts and sandals on both occasions. He also ran a marathon in the Namib desert without drinking water. One of the key elements of his practices is the so-called Wim Hof Method, where you take around 30 quick, deep breaths with subsequent holding of your breath for usually three rounds, before immersing yourself in cold water for a few minutes.

Several studies have been undertaken to evaluate the impacts of cold exposure on different health conditions. The application for professional athletes around the reduction of delayed onset muscle soreness after exercise is fairly well established[16]. Other benefits revolve around immune enhancement[17] and fat loss[18]. However, enhancement of brain function and mood are what I believe to be the most important benefits of this exercise.

---

16. Stacey et al. (2010): Effects of recovery method after exercise on performance, immune changes, and psychological outcomes

17. Sevchuk, Radoja (2007): Possible stimulation of anti-tumor immunity using repeated cold stress: a hypothesis;undefinedMooventhan, Nivethitha (2014): Scientific evidence-based effects of hydrotherapy on various systems of the body andundefinedBuijze at al. (2016): The effects of cold showering on health and work: a randomised controlled trial

18. Coolbaugh at al. (2019): Cold exposure induces dynamic, heterogenous alterations in human brown adipose tissue lipid content

Exposure to cold is known to stimulate beta-endorphins and norepinephrines[19]. Norepinephrine is one of the key factors involved in depression. It involves regulation of focus, mood, motivation, attention and intellect[20]. For example in people suffering from ADHD, altered Norepinephrine processing can be observed[21]. Higher levels of these chemicals might explain, why the exposure to cold appears to be a promising treatment for relieving symptoms of depression[22].

There is something else that I would like to discuss in this space. Taking a cold shower or an ice bath is stressful for the body and it has to respond to the potential danger of cold. For example, it does so by restricting the blood flow, especially to the extremities (the hands and feet) to save energy for where it matters the most - keeping the torso and the organs warm. Once you are warming up again, blood vessels are dilated and blood flow will increase accordingly. This whole thing is basically a "stress exercise" for the body in a (mostly) safe manner. Imagine how powerful you could feel after regularly starting a day with an exercise where you learn to deal with stress by:

1. having to jump over your shadow and turn the shower to

---

19. Shevchuk (2007): Adapted cold shower as a potential treatment for depression

20. Moret, Briley (2011): The importance of norepinephrine in depression

21. Faraone et al. (2014): Biomarkers in the diagnosis of ADHD - promising directions

22. Rymaszewska et al. (2008): Whole-body cryotherapy as adjunct treatment of depressive and anxiety disorders
and
Porges (2010): Stress and Parasympathetic Control.

cold or immerse yourself in the cold water and

2. managing to recover and feeling well after the (physically) stressful encounter

I feel like this can provide higher resilience to other stress-inducing environments and situations in life. The intensity of the experience also switches your attention directly to your bodily sensations. This comes with plenty of benefits already discussed in the sections around yoga and consciousness.

I feel like a piece of shit today. Is there any reason for it? Work is going well. My social life is going well. There are no specific experiences or thoughts that I have to resolve. I've had enough sleep and have been eating well. So there is no magic story behind why I feel this way. Or is there? Maybe I'm just not seeing it. Maybe on some days I'm just not well. After all, emotions are unpredictable. They are also passing. Like clouds, remember. Maybe it's just chemicals? I want to at least do what is in my power before I accept this state of being. Good thing there is a cheat code: Exposure to cold.

I know that nothing bad can happen to me. I have done this before. But this time it's ice? Actual ice. I have to break through it to gain access to this pond. I'm still scared. What if it's just too cold. Is there such a thing as sudden unexpected grownup death syndrome? Because life was just... too cold? Actually, in the seventies, there was something called sudden unexpected nocturnal death syndrome among Laotian immigrants in the US. They fled from Lao after the communist movement Pathet Lao came into power. The best explanation that scientists could come up with was the following: In the United States, they lacked the shamanic protection rituals from a make-believe nocturnal demon called the 'dab tsog'. Their belief in dab tsog was apparently strong enough for them to wake up with sleep paralysis. The subsequent panic was sufficiently intense to cause their heart to stop beating[23]. Ok ok ok, stop it Fred! I'm not worried about the dab tsog, and I'm doing this in broad daylight. So I should be fine, right? Right? It's just going to be cold for a moment and then I'll be happy, that's all there is to it. I have done my three sets of breathing exercises and the oven inside is lit already, therefore it will keep me nice and warm once I'm done here. So, I slowly step into the pond until the water is up to my hips. There is no turning back now. [Don't listen to that, you can always turn back!] Anyways, I go in further until I'm neck-deep in the pond. My body starts hyperventilating and breathing rapidly. Regulate it, Fred! Slow it down! That's what Wim Hof said to do, remember? Deep, slow breaths. After a few seconds, I manage to calm the breathing down. From here onwards, it's a breeze. My body feels like it's levitating. I have extreme clarity of mind. I feel alive. There is me, the observer. Calm, existing, loving. And there is the body, the observed. I can feel the life flowing through it, being slowed down and calmed by the cold. What a gift. A part of me just wants to stay here and enjoy it for a little longer. However, I haven't done it many times yet so I don't want to push it. Once my timer rings after four minutes, I get out. After drying myself quickly, I put on several layers of clothing and stand in front of the fireplace to warm up again. I can feel my blood circulation rebooting throughout my body; my hands and feet have that fizzing sensation you get when you come back home from

23. Robson (2022): The expectation effect, p. 18

sledding or skiing on a cold winter's day. I can also feel the hormone cocktail of happiness doing its work in my brain. I'm alive. I trust the natural flow of life. I feel like I could tackle any problem right now. Oh yeah. What a cheat.

Chapter Six

Negative Thoughts

Psychoeducation and cognitive behavioural therapy - gaining a rational understanding of what is going on[1]

I find great comfort in the thought that emotions and behavior, at their core, make sense. Understanding where we come from and the impact our childhoods have on our lives helps incredibly in finding solutions and dealing with our experiences. Our bodies and our emotions are telling us stories, sometimes obvious ones, sometimes ones

---

1. See Walker (2013): Complex PTSD, p. 36ff, p. 55ff. If this chapter speaks to you, I highly recommend directly reading Walker's work

that are harder to uncover and to resolve. We can listen, understand and act accordingly. Reading this book for example is a good step of "psychoeducating" yourself. However, as important as this cognitive understanding of trauma is, unfortunately there is a good chance that this alone will not be sufficient. Generally, it's best to address all levels of trauma and microtrauma - including the physical and emotional ones, also discussed throughout this part of the book.

Ideally, cognitive behavioral therapy (CBT) supports you in understanding your past, your protective patterns in response to this past as well as what self-compassionate and self-protective behavior would look like instead. Questions like:

- *"Why am I feeling this way?"*

- *"How can I set healthy boundaries towards others?"* or

- *"How can I express explicit compassion for my own well-being?"*

should find their answer here.

This relates to an aspect that I particularly like about the potential benefits of CBT - reparenting, which includes re-mothering and re-fathering. In this context, motherly love[2] is supposed to be unconditionally affectionate towards the infant. Freud called this phase *"his majesty the baby"*[3]. On the other hand, fatherly love has the role of slowly introducing boundaries to the growing child, while also protecting it. As outlined in earlier sections, these stances are internal-

---

2. See Fromm (1956): "The Art of Loving" for a nice elaboration of these concepts

3. Freud (1914): On Narcissism: An Introduction

ized by the child. Ideally while growing up, it develops an instinct of self-compassion and a deep sense of being deserving of love in response to unconditional motherly affection. The internalization of fatherly love should lead to an instinct of self-protection and deep understanding of setting boundaries, while also being able to respect the needs of others. Now, if we grew up in environments where we weren't shown these qualities to a good enough degree, we can "reparent" ourselves at a later point in time. Adult experiences and relations can serve as examples for what this healthy stance towards oneself could look like.

> *Therapy allowed me to internalize and mimic my therapists' consistent and reliable stance of being on my side.*

> Pete Walker[4]

The dynamic of "healthy narcissism" in therapy, where the therapist gives you their undivided and unconditional positive attention, can serve as a prime experience of self-mothering. This includes being accepting of yourself in all stances and being self-nurturing in regards to all your core needs, be they verbal, spiritual, emotional or physical.

Psychoeducation and CBT can also help with a better understanding of negative beliefs and the inner child. Combining this understanding of yourself with an increased level of consciousness will develop the skill of observing our inner self-commentary. This is an incredibly important step towards replacing any negative thoughts with

---

4. Walker (2013): Complex PTSD, p. 58

a more self-compassionate and self-protective stance. It is also a wonderful basis for deep intimacy in relationships. Being able to notice and authentically open up about all aspects of our experience - including the difficult ones, potentially considered shameful or embarrassing - will significantly increase the sense of belonging and acceptance found in any relationship.

Healing negative beliefs, tending to the inner child and establishing a positive concept of self

Here is a quick recap from the beliefs sections above: Basically, we learn how to treat ourselves from our caregivers and environment. We keep on treating ourselves like this even long after we have moved out from home. Negative beliefs show themselves in adult life as criticism or shame, for example in the form of perfectionism, guilt, workaholism, catastrophizing or name-calling. For an improvement in quality of life, it is important to work on these negative beliefs.

A holistic recovery process ideally contains the following elements:

- Working on our negative beliefs and shrinking them

- Learning to express our emotions, including grieving and angering

- Learning to experience all physical sensations and working with our bodies

It usually makes sense to start with beliefs, as some negative beliefs are on a meta level. They don't just lead us to unnecessarily reject ourselves, but they do it in a way that prevents us from doing any other recovery work first. *"Nothing I do ever works"*, *"I don't deserve happiness"*, *"crying means being weak"*, *"girls always have to be proper. They shouldn't make a scene or stir things up"*, or *"therapy is for sick people, not for me"* are examples for negative beliefs that work on a meta level and might prevent psychoeducation, psychological progress and healthily expressing our emotions. The belief that you can develop your abilities and your life through effort and hard work is crucial. It should be ensured or established first to allow for the following recovery work.

> *Self-acceptance is my refusal to be in an adversarial*
> *relationship to myself*

> Nathaniel Branden

It is perfectly natural and ok that some experiences are overwhelming, no matter the circumstances. In most cases, the root of behavior comes from such a young age where it's perfectly natural to be helpless. What were we supposed to do as one year olds? Educate our parents how to love us properly? Set boundaries? Imagine that... no I think we are never to blame for the things that happen(ed) to us. We can however slowly and steadily change the outcome and work on how we feel about life and ourselves. It's okay to be struggling, to ask for help, to go to therapy or to start new things that frighten us. Life comes at us in waves and there will always be times where it's a little harder and that's okay. Two steps forward, one step back. Thoughts like these should serve as enablers on a meta level. They help us to start taking measures like buying the book, doing the exercise or starting the therapy we've had in mind for a while.

Sometimes I just feel Irrelephant

Thought-stopping and substitution to shrink negative beliefs

Here we need to apply the "observing ego" function. It refers to the ability to step outside of ourselves and observe our emotions, motivations and actions.It can be trained and improved by looking at difficult situations in the aftermath and observing how we felt and what we thought. The better we get, the closer we can get to observing these things in real time - even in the "heat of the moment" and then adapting our response right there and then. We could stop ourselves in the self-condemning thoughts and replace them to be more aligned with positive beliefs, self-compassion and self-protection.

Back when Mirco the second, my little scooter at the time, was in power, I had returned to Vienna from my landscaping stint. I waited tables to get by. At university, I was about to finish my undergrad in Landscape Architecture. I had somehow managed to complete almost the entire curriculum. Only my thesis and one exam was left. The project work to get there was mostly doable. Exams were still incredibly difficult for me, though. For most of them, I would sit there the night before and study at the last minute. Only on the two or three occasions where I failed, would I start preparing well in advance on the second try. But preparing in advance for standard deadlines? No way. Pulling all-nighters to meet deadlines or projects or for exams remained a semi-regular occurrence.

Regarding my thesis: I've got my concept, I've conducted my research. I've even received blessings for my research design and methodology. In terms of writing the whole thing down, I maybe have around two thirds by now. There is only one problem: the deadline is tomorrow. In about 17 hours, to be more precise. My mood is based on discipline and focus in the face of adversity. I'm a warrior! What adversity though? My own adversity? I could have easily spent more time on this over the last six weeks. Yes, I'm a little busier these days with work, dating and friends, but that's no excuse. Are we all just our own greatest enemies? Are my dragons still looming, always just waiting for the next deadline before they come out of their cage? By 2am, my discipline and focus are starting to dwindle. I'm not even halfway through the missing chapters yet. I wonder if the fourth energy drink in the midst of an all-nighter will have any beneficial effect. I can feel my heart pounding against my chest, as if saying, "Let me out! Make it stop! I have worked enough today!" The drinks are certainly having some effect on me. I'm just not sure if it's actually beneficial. For fuck's sake. I want to go to sleep. Why did it have to come to this again? Have I learned nothing in the last three years? Fucking idiot. What the hell am I doing here? Oi! Stop it! Right there! There is no need to put myself down like this. Or to be this harsh to myself. Two steps forward, one step back. Tonight is a step back. But I just have to bite the bullet for a few more hours. And then I can finish my degree. Wouldn't that be a leap forward, after all the fuckery of the last few years? And there is no computer in sight. I don't have to play on the computer to distract myself from the "pain" of studying or writing for an hour. All is well. I can still finish this in time. Go easy on yourself! Much love!

And I did finish in time. I completed the writing by 7am, got feedback by 9am, wrapped the document up by 11am and then had 3 hours left to add the list of citations, burn it on a CD, print it, bind it, make my way to university and deliver it in the seminar at 2pm. Up until today, it was the last all-nighter I ever pulled for a deadline.

Negative beliefs can also be about others instead of ourselves, such as when you have the feeling that everyone just lets you down or is flawed or unhelpful. As well as people, they can be about the outside world and life in general. Negative beliefs about others isolate others from ourselves (*"everyone is stupid"*) while negative beliefs about ourselves isolate us from others (*"I'm not good enough for others"*). In reality, all of them lead to isolation in a way that is not self-compassionate or self-loving.

Huge thanks to Pete Walker for letting me show his slightly adapted Toolbox about negative beliefs here[5]. If this speaks to you, I encourage you to read more of his material:

Toolbox - Suggested internal responses to common internal attacks

The attacks of negative beliefs operate below the radar of self-awareness. Unless we can identify them, we are at their mercy and helpless to deconstruct them. Once we learn to recognize them, the simple techniques of Thought-Stopping and Thought-Substitution are powerful tools. There are two categories of attacks. Perfectionism attacks, fueled by toxic shame, create chronic self-hate and self-flagellation. Endangerment attacks, fueled by fear, create chronic hypervigilance and anxiety.

PERFECTIONISM ATTACKS

1. **Perfectionism**. My perfectionism arose as an attempt to gain safety and support in my dangerous family. Perfection is a self-persecutory myth. I do not have to be perfect to be safe or loved in the present. I am letting go of relationships that require perfection. I have a right to make mistakes. Mistakes do not make me a mistake. Every mistake or mishap is an opportunity to practice loving myself in the places I have never been loved.

---

5. Walker, 2013: Complex PTSD, p. 202, 203

2. **All-or-None & Black-and-White Thinking.** I reject extreme or over generalized descriptions, judgments or criticisms. Statements that describe me as "always" or "never" this or that, are typically grossly inaccurate.

3. **Self-Hate, Self-Disgust & Toxic Shame.** I commit to myself. I am on my side. I am a good enough person. I refuse to trash myself. I turn shame back into blame and disgust and externalize it to anyone who shames my normal feelings and foibles. As long as I am not hurting anyone, I refuse to be shamed for normal emotional responses like anger, sadness, fear and depression. I especially refuse to attack myself for how hard it is to completely eliminate the self-hate habit.

4.   **Micromanagement/Worrying/Obsessing/Looping/Over-Futurizing**. I will not repetitively examine details over and over. I will not endlessly second-guess myself. I cannot change the past. I forgive all my past mistakes. I cannot make the future perfectly safe. I will stop hunting for what could go wrong. I will not try to control the uncontrollable. I will not micromanage myself or others. I work in a way that is "good enough", and I accept the existential fact that my efforts sometimes bring desired results and sometimes they do not. "God grant me the serenity to accept the things I cannot change, the courage to change the things I can, and the wisdom to know the difference".

5. **Unfair/Devaluing Comparisons to others or to your most perfect moments.** I refuse to compare myself unfavorably to others. I will not compare "my insides to their outsides". I will not judge myself for not being at peak performance all of the time. In a society that pressures us into acting happy all the time, I will not get down on myself for feeling bad.

6. **Guilt**. Feeling guilty does not mean I am guilty. I refuse to make my decisions and choices out of guilt; sometimes I need to feel the guilt

and do it anyway. In the inevitable instance when I inadvertently hurt someone, I will apologize, make amends, and let go of my guilt. I will not apologize over and over. I am no longer a victim. I will not accept unfair blame. Guilt is sometimes camouflaged fear: "I am afraid, but I am not guilty or in danger".

7. **Shoulding**. I will substitute the words "want to" for "should" and only follow this imperative if it feels like I want to, unless I am under legal, ethical or moral obligation.

8. **Over-Productivity/Workaholism/Busyholism**. I am a human being not a human doing. I will not choose to be perpetually productive. In the long run, I am more productive when I balance work with play and relaxation. I will not try to perform at 100% all the time. I subscribe to the normalcy of vacillating along a continuum of efficiency.

9. **Harsh Judgments of Self & Others/Name-Calling**. I will not let the bullies and critics of my early life win by joining and agreeing with them. I refuse to attack myself or abuse others. I will not displace the criticism and blame that rightfully belongs to my original critics onto myself or current people in my life. "I care for myself. The more solitary, the more friendless, the more unsustained I am, the more I will respect myself". - Jane Eyre

ENDANGERMENT ATTACKS

10. **Drasticizing/Catastrophizing/Hypochondriasizing**. I feel afraid but I am not in danger. I am not "in trouble" with my parents. I refuse to scare myself with thoughts and pictures of my life deteriorating. No more home-made horror movies and disaster flicks. No more turning tiny ailments into tales of dying.

11. **Negative focus**. I will stop anxiously looking for, over-noticing and dwelling on what might go wrong or what might be wrong with

me or life around me. Right now, I will notice, visualize and enumerate my accomplishments, talents and qualities, as well as the many gifts life offers me, like music, film, food, beauty, color, books, nature, friends, etc.

12. **Time Urgency**. I am not in danger. I do not need to rush. I will not hurry unless it is a true emergency. I am learning to enjoy doing my daily activities at a relaxed pace.

13. **Disabling Performance Anxiety**. I am reducing procrastination by reminding myself not to accept unfair criticism or perfectionist expectations from anyone. Even when afraid, I will defend myself from unfair criticism. I won't let fear make my decisions.

14. **Perseverating About Being Attacked**. Unless there are clear signs of danger, I will thoughtstop my projection of past bullies/critics onto others. The majority of my fellow human beings are peaceful people. I have legal authorities to aid in my protection if threatened by the few who aren't. I invoke thoughts and images of my friends' love and support

Chapter Seven

Positive Thoughts

Grass doesn't grow quicker when you pull it

Recovery takes a lot of time and effort, and sometimes it feels like we still fall back into our old emotional habits despite consistently working on ourselves. I think it's really important to be patient with ourselves and any progress we make. There are a few neuroscientific insights that have really helped me accept the pace of slow and gradual progress.

The brain learns with associations that are built by our experiences. Think of the classic Pavlovian dog, the bowl of food and the bell. If the bell is rung any time the dog is being served his food, the dog will then start associating a ringing bell with his mealtime. He will anticipate food, even when the bell rings but no food is actually being served. If the bell has been rung hundreds or thousands of times together with food being served, the connection will obviously be much stronger than if it has just happened a couple of times. Similarly, think of hearing criticism every time we make a minor mistake. We will build a strong connection between screwing up and having to criticize ourselves. This plays into the internalization of parenting discussed earlier. In terms of neurological paths, think of a large, wide open field in a cold winter that has been covered in snow up to our knees. If we only walk over it once, we might make a path that quickly disappears the next time it snows.

However, if we walk the same path routinely as it maybe leads us to the nearest supermarket or the city center, we will build a clearer, stronger path. Maybe others will join us, until at some point, we actually build a proper footpath, or a road. More and more people might use it, until it turns into a full six-lane highway. Now let's get back to our example - a trigger situation. We make a little mistake. The brain might have learned in childhood that even minor mistakes lead to being criticized. There is a fully built highway leading from "making a minor mistake" over to "being criticized". So, even if no one is there to criticize you, your brain is still inclined to take the way over to self-criticism and self-shaming. After all, there is a fully built highway while all around it are just snowy fields. And this is where our work around positive beliefs, thought-stopping and thought-substitution comes in. Through the snow, we make a new path from *"making a minor mistake"* to *"it's okay to make mistakes. I am worthy of love nonetheless".* The first time you take that path, you might find that it gets lost in the snow. But if you consistently take that way, it will sooner or later turn into an actual paved road that is more and more common for your brain to use. And upon being used less and less, the old path will start to wither. It will slowly be taken over by nature, given enough time.

So it takes a lot of work, patience and "rewiring" to end up with the consistently self-compassionate and self-protective way of thinking that we all deserve. Go easy on yourself in times of falling back into old habits, or when it feels like you're not making enough progress. Think about where you were when you started this journey and the changes you have already accomplished.

What to aim for

I feel like the work of Nathaniel Branden[1] in the area of self-esteem is too important not to mention it here. I want to share his definition of self-esteem that runs in both directions along the axis of interaction between ourselves and the outside world. It includes a positive understanding of our own capabilities to deal with the world as well as our own entitlement to good things happening to us from "the outside". In his own words, self-esteem is:

1. confidence in our ability to think, confidence in our ability to cope with the basic challenges of life; and

2. confidence in our right to be successful and happy, the feeling of being worthy, deserving, entitled to assert our needs and wants, achieve our values, and enjoy the fruits of our efforts.[2]

In Branden's eyes, building self-esteem requires more than just reciting positive self-affirmations. It presents an achievement that we actively have to work for. You might find principles, actions and chapters throughout this book that resemble Branden's pillars of self-esteem (consciousness, authenticity or purpose, among others). For now, I want to focus on the understanding of what self-esteem actually means. What it is we are aiming for when crafting positive beliefs or when we are observing and stopping our negative beliefs. It is the absolute conviction that we are generally capable of dealing with life while being compassionate enough to know that we are worthy of and deserve all the good things that come our way. For example, when working with these concepts, I realized that I am generally convinced that I'm resilient and capable of doing well in life, while I severely

---

1. Branden (1994): The six pillars of self-esteem. See also: Branden (1972): The disowned self

2. Branden (1994): The six pillars of self-esteem, p. 4

lacked the entitlement to being treated well, to looking out for my own good or even enjoying life in general. It was a completely new experience and skill I had to learn to ask myself things like: what would I genuinely enjoy doing right now? How could I treat myself well tonight? Oftentimes, these are different things than what we are inclined to do. Cooking myself a good meal or taking a relaxing bath certainly makes me feel better than ordering takeout or just having a quick shower. However, it also takes a conscious effort of self-care to do so. For other people it might be different, or the other way around - they could protect themselves or treat themselves well while questioning their own capabilities to do well in life.

Establishing positive beliefs[3]

What you have read so far can hopefully serve as good inspiration for what positive beliefs can look like. The leading principles of positive beliefs usually revolve around self-protection, self-compassion and self-acceptance, so generally everything that highlights ourselves as being our own greatest ally. Ideally, you already have a rough idea of negative beliefs from your childhood. So in line with the exercise shown in the trauma section, you might be aware of key words, typical sentences said to you, or a certain role you might have had in your family. Now we want to identify existing positive beliefs. For this we can also go back to our past, our parents or our caregivers and think about any positive messages we received or any positive outlooks on

---

3. See also: Stahl, 2020: The Child in You: The Breakthrough Method for Bringing Out Your Authentic Self

life that we adapted and internalized. For example, I always considered myself to be incredibly resilient and able to withstand the strongest of storms. Or maybe you had a grandma that was always super relaxed and forgiving and radiated an *"it's okay - you are always welcome, no matter what happens"* kind of vibe.

We also want to find positive "counterparts" for the negative beliefs that have been identified already. Here it's important to not use any negations (like in *"I am not a burden"*) but use direct, affirmative messages. *"I am a burden"* could for example turn into *"it's okay to be a burden sometimes"* or to *"I am welcomed"*. Other examples for positive beliefs could be:

- I am okay the way I am

- I am good enough

- I am loved

- I am capable

- It's okay to make mistakes

- It's okay to set boundaries

- I'm allowed to feel and express my feelings

- It's okay to ask for help or go to therapy

- I will be okay, no matter what happens

I really like the thought that things don't need to be perfect. You don't need to be perfect, and neither do your parents, your friends or your partners. Also neither does your job, your financial situation or your life in general. It just has to be *good enough*. It's entirely okay if you are just good *enough*. For me, that includes having reasonably good intentions and *trying* to do well. I really like the forgiving aspect of this, especially in the context of self-development. Our emotional experience is frequently changing and unpredictable. It is not something we can choose. No emotional state can be induced to persist as a permanent experience. It's okay to make mistakes or to feel down sometimes - let's cut ourselves some slack!

This principle of "good enough" is also extremely helpful for all decision making in life. We will go into more general aspects of decision making later on. For now it's just important to note the principle of good enough in decision making. This can apply to minor decisions like picking the right jam in the supermarket: I don't need to find the best jam among 30 options, I just need to find one that fulfills my criteria, like no pieces of fruit and not too much sugar. My life will generally be more satisfying if I get a jam that is "good enough" instead of worrying and spending time in search of the best possible jam among so many different options. Funnily enough, the same goes for larger, more important life decisions, like finding a job or choosing a partner. What would my life look like if I always tried to find the best possible option on the market? Imagine trying to find the best possible needle in a three hundred million haystack! For me it's just about finding a solution that's good enough. Of course, what is good enough will have ambitious criteria for more important decisions. I want my relationships to be stable, loving and fun. However, no relationship is going to be perfect; so instead of asking myself "could I find something better out there?" I prefer sticking to the question "can I live with this, enjoy it and accept it?".

Let's get a bit more practical in this space - what are your positive beliefs? What are the positive counterparts to your negative beliefs? Feel free to grab a pen and paper and see what you can come up with!

I feel like this is also a good moment to come up with and capture our positive traits, our resources, our reserves - all of the good things about our life. In times of crisis we sometimes resort to all-or-none thinking and forget how many positive things there are that could support us or that we have achieved or experienced. It's best to write these down when not in crisis, so you can remember them or read up on them in more difficult times. This might include friends, good habits, achievements, pleasant experiences, personality traits or physical resources like an apartment or beautiful nature around you..

Allow me to share my own key positive beliefs - I feel like they relate well to my overall story and I love reading through all of them every now and then to make sure I am not going in the wrong direction. Occasionally, I can also see that some are particularly relevant to the problems I might currently be facing.

- I am a lovable man

- I deserve my own, unconditional love and affection

- My presence is welcomed

- My worth is based purely on my existence. I am love. I am worthy of love

- I am a fully grown, mature man

- I am the author of my own reality

- You are a guest in my reality

- Love, gratitude, humbleness

- I trust the general flow of life

- I am safe

- I am responsible for my own feelings

- I am allowed to set boundaries

- Noone else can "make" me happy or sad

- I will be okay

- It is okay to slack sometimes

Humour

Olivia suddenly gets a call, gets up and leaves the room to talk. The others, Liam and Emma, also friends of mine, quickly enlighten me that it's Olivia's dad calling. He forgot her birthday yesterday and it's a sensitive topic as it wasn't for the first time. Once she gets back, the mood in the room is a little... tense. Wanting to lighten the mood, I tell her "I feel you, my dad hasn't called me on my birthday in 26 years". Without missing a beat, she responds, "Let me guess, he went to buy milk and never came back?" The pure sass. I love it. While I am still shocked at her witty response, Liam looks at her with a completely straight face and shoots back with a dry, serious tone of voice, "No, he's dead". Boom! You know the acronym ROFL - Rolling on the floor laughing? It was made for situations like these; I couldn't keep myself on the chair anymore. I was laughing, gasping for air and crying because I was laughing so hard. All of a sudden, a slightly awkward and tense mood in the room had been resolved and Olivia was able to laugh at her misfortune. Of course, this requires me to "read the room" and calibrate carefully what I'm bringing to it. It also requires me to be completely comfortable with something as personal as my father's passing to use it as material for humorous situations. There is something about humor in the face of dire situations that helps in making them more bearable. Let's have a closer look.

The psychiatrist George Vaillant classifies humor as a mature defense mechanism, usually found among healthy, successful humans[4]. It is more commonly used as a coping mechanism in professions that have to deal with potentially traumatic incidents on a regular basis, like firefighters or paramedics[5]. I think its therapeutic value lies in the application of the positive belief that *"I will be ok, no matter what".* It radiates a certain acceptance of the situation. The term "gallows humor" literally originates from people being humorous in the face of their certain death at the gallows. William Palmer, for example, hanged in 1856, supposedly looked at the trapdoor on the gallows and asked the hangman *"are you sure it's safe?"* Imagine that - radiating acceptance and "I will be okay" even in the face of certain death. How powerful is that? In his essay about humor, Freud calls this

---

4. Vaillant (1994): Ego mechanisms of defence and personality psychopathology

5. See e.g. Christopher (2015): An introduction to black humour as a coping mechanism for student paramedics

"*the victorious assertion of the ego's invulnerability. The ego refuses to be distressed by the provocations of reality, to let itself be compelled to suffer*".[6] Furthermore, he goes on that humor just wants to say: "*Look! Here is the world, which seems so dangerous! It is nothing but a game for children-just worth making a jest about!*" This is directly related to and dependent on the definition of "I", which we want to discuss in the second part of this book. We will see that there is a definition of the "I" or the ego, where it is possible to be convinced of "I will be okay" even in the face of certain death.

There is also the perspective of evolutionary biology. We want to communicate to the brain that we are safe, and what better way than using pathways and mechanisms that are most likely millions of years old?[7] Generally, laughter serves the function of forging social bonds in groups quickly and effectively. As the alternative - physical touch - is somewhat difficult to maintain with more than two or three people simultaneously over longer periods of time. A precondition to doing this, however, is that the basic necessities of life are covered, resources are available and that you are not in immediate danger. So humor and laughter were historically only applied in periods of safety and satiation. Gervais and Wilson argue that, as a consequence, humor (or non-serious social incongruity as they call it) "*would have been a reliable indicator of such safe times*".[8] So basically your brain hears: "*Humor? Nice. That must mean that I'm safe. Otherwise we wouldn't be laughing and joking around*".

---

6. Freud (1927): Humour

7. See: Scott (2015): TED Talk "Why we laugh"

8. Gervais, Wilson (2005): The evolution and functions of laughter and humor: a synthetic approach

So, thinking of our overall healing dynamics postulated in the beginning of the healing section, I think that being able to joke about troubling affairs can on the one hand establish an immediate sense of safety and competence, but on the other, also be a powerful tool in your toolbox for long-term integration and mastery of your experiences. Personally, I certainly experience traumatic incidents less regularly than professions like firefighters or paramedics; however I find humor to be extremely helpful in difficult conversations and topics. It aids me in illustrating to myself, to my partner or to friends, that things are okay and are going to be okay, even if one of us is stuck in a trauma-based flashback way of thinking. It also helps in lightening the mood after intimate discussions in partnerships by boldly using my own "sensitive spots" as material for subsequent humor.

Chapter Eight

Short-term Safety and Long-term Mastery

Expressing yourself to successfully integrate painful experiences

Let's have another look at the three steps introduced at the beginning of Part II:

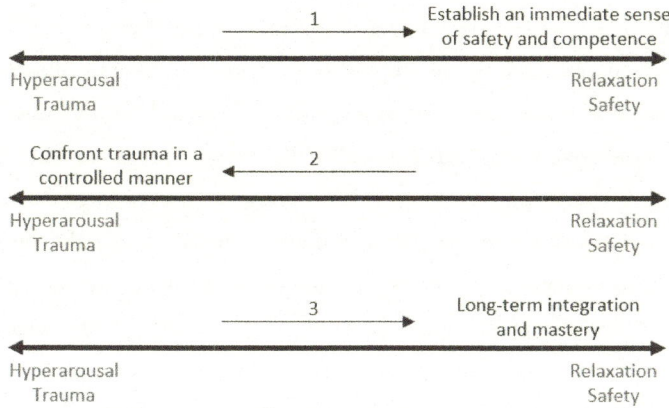

In this chapter, we're going to take a closer look at "moving" along the line, in all three steps shown above, specifically in relation to challenging or traumatic experiences and events. We will look at possible ways to confront trauma in a controlled manner, establishing an immediate sense of safety as well as subsequent healing, integration and mastery. Once the skills for step three are built in the long term, we can also improve our action in step one in the "present tense" to directly resolve challenging situations as much as possible. Realizing these opportunities in the heat of the moment, and not just in the aftermath, requires a lot of practice to achieve.

Before we begin: confronting traumatic experiences can be extremely overwhelming. It bears the danger of retraumatizing yourself, instead of resolving the experience. If you are scared of that happening, I recommend that you only (re-)confront traumatic experiences with the support of qualified, professional help.

Peter Levine and Bessel van der Kolk[1] came up with the principle of *pendulation* - to safely and repeatedly move into accessing memories and sensations within the window of tolerance (step 2 in the illustration above), and then move back out of them to the "here and now", to a feeling of safety (step 3 above). With progress and capacity building over time, one can increase the window of tolerance, go deeper into these memories and express the physical impulses and fight/flight responses that were suppressed during the traumatic incidents. This *pendulation* happens between arousal and safety, between the dangerous past and the safe present and between exploring stored tensions in the body and anchoring oneself in the current environment.

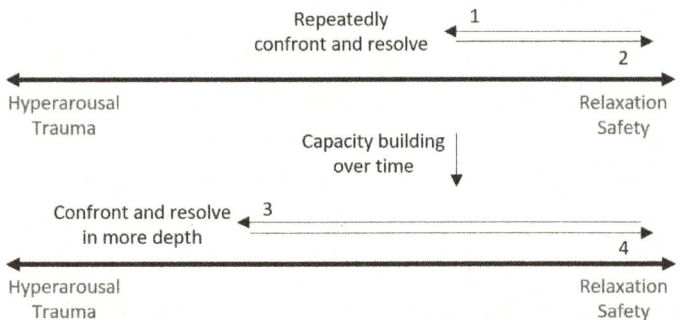

Levine and van der Kolk primarily use this concept in body-based therapies like sensorimotor psychotherapy and somatic experiencing[2]. However, I would like to include options for confrontation that are less body-oriented, like verbal ventilation or artistic expression, such as writing or painting. For me, it's about confronting something uncomfortable (confrontation) and then simulating to the brain a

---

1. Van der Kolk (2015): The body keeps the score, p.233

2. E.g. Ogden, Fisher (2014): Sensorimotor Psychotherapy; quoted in van der Kolk (2015): The body keeps the score p. 235

successful fight/flight response that would take it back to safety (expression). This is supposed to allow us to "experience the experience" and let it become a part of the past, instead of carrying it with us and allowing it to become part of our filter (as described in the trauma section). As with prior input in the space of trauma research and scientific insights, I want to think about how to break down and apply these principles to any situation that is challenging, like a breakup, a heated discussion or an encounter with a bear.

Confrontation

Confrontation with the uncomfortable experience happens with action that pulls the experience back into our scope of consciousness. On one side we have the physically-oriented, "working directly with the body"- type of therapies mentioned above. While on the other hand, one can start confronting the experience in a more abstract manner, like writing. Feeling, thinking, speaking about something, or using another artistic expression like painting, can also be helpful along this process of confrontation. Writing about upsetting events has shown to improve mental and physical health in various circumstances, such as with nursing home residents, students or prisoners[3]. It is important to be okay with acknowledging, accessing, and accepting feelings like anger or sadness, without running into negative beliefs on a meta-level like *"crying shows weakness"* and *"I have to control my anger"*. It's okay to feel all emotions. Anger, sadness, fear, shame, and

---

3. Van der Kolk (2015): The body keeps the score, p. 257

depression - they serve their purpose. They tell stories, they want to be heard! It is also helpful to direct any output first and foremost to yourself to prevent social guards from interfering with your thought processes. If you are happy and comfortable with your output, you can still share it afterwards. Directly writing something to address someone else and to share with them makes it more difficult to freely access what you truly feel about the experience.

Whatever you write about, to include the emotions and feelings connected to the experiences will greatly improve the result[50]. Regarding topics to write about, there are several possible routes to take. You can start with any object around you, combined with free association and then delve into the memories, feelings and daydreams that start coming up. You'll be surprised where you can end up by simply starting off like this. You could write about early childhood emotions and patterns that have been discussed in earlier sections, as well as about specific traumatic incidents or recent challenging experiences. I personally like using writing to explore my emotions in relation to very specific incidents and patterns, be it from childhood or from my current life.

There are two acts that are particularly important for the success of this practice: angering and crying. Pete Walker describes anger as *"aggressively complaining about current or past losses and injustices"*[4]. It creates healthy resentment against actions that inflicted pain, as well as against betrayal and against a lack of guidance and protection. It awakens our life spirits to actively and aggressively lament what happened. It helps us in developing the self-protective stance and fatherly love towards ourselves that is so important in bringing to life the "we deserve good things"- part of self-esteem. It is best directed against

---

4. Walker (2013): Complex PTSD, p. 149

the internalized parents and the negative beliefs in action. It can also be (mentally, in writing) directed against aggressors in recent or past experiences to at least mentally voice the assertion of our boundaries. The better we become at awaking and expressing this anger in hindsight, the more we will be able to protect our boundaries in the present moment and prevent painful experiences from happening in the first place.

Crying can dissolve fear, shame and the feeling of abandonment. It soothes and triggers the relaxation response of our parasympathetic nervous system. In crying, we can learn to feel the self-compassion that is so critical in feeling worthy of love. We can greatly benefit from mourning what we never received. The lack of space, parental care or affection that we so desperately needed as children; the missing social inclusion, belonging and connection at school or in adult life; our boundaries and our self-worth not being respected in situations that were extremely hurtful. Mourning things like the loss of a happy childhood or the loss of our feeling of safety and integrity can help us in resolving our experiences. It can help us in accepting the way things have turned out.

It's best to let both - crying and angering - happen. If we only allow one to take place, we run the risk of getting stuck in an endless cycle of whining or complaining, where one of the two gets suppressed and never resolved. Unfortunately there is a lot of societal compartmentalization that takes place, such as assigning anger to men and crying to women. Things like "*a good lady does not show her anger*" or "*only weak men cry*" are absolutely detrimental for a healthy, holistic process of resolving traumatic experiences.

Personally, I was reprimanded time and time again for any expressions of anger. From today's perspective, it was a helpless child's desperate attempt to draw attention to an abusive environment. I was diagnosed with ADHD, medicated against my will and branded a "difficult" child by caregivers, psychiatrists and teachers alike because I was so eager to be loud, to receive attention, to be heard. I was framed as a problem that needs to be silenced and that "*must learn to behave*". I skipped school at the age of 6, got into physical fights with peers at the age of 9 and into heated arguments with teachers at the age of 11. I despised their incompetence in dealing with mobbing and was not afraid to tell them that. I was also punished for any signs of aggression. When my classmate pulled down my pants, humiliating me in front of 50 peers, my response was to physically hit him in the stomach. I received the same punishment as him for my act of (slightly misguided) self-defence. I was consistently taught to suppress my anger and let it out as sadness. I learned that quietly crying myself to sleep at night under the blanket got me into less trouble than voicing my anger towards peers or caregivers. Subsequently, for a good 15 years, my pretty much only response to me being hurt or my boundaries being crossed was crying and sadness. I had to learn over several years with countless therapy sessions, writings and reflections to let a healthy anger thrive and come out. To learn to not suppress my aggression and have it turn to sadness before I realise what's going on. To feel the love and the power in protecting myself. You do not cross me. Noone does. I don't take no crap no more. Nice. Setting boundaries successfully is so empowering. In 2019, one dark December evening would put my capabilities in healthy expression of anger to the test quite substantially, but more about that later.

Immediate Safety

After confronting an uncomfortable experience, the goal is to re-establish a sense of safety. This is supposed to illustrate to your brain that the uncomfortable experience has passed and you are now safe. Doing so will lead to two things:

1. Capacity building. It increases your window of tolerance in the face of uncomfortable situations. With increasing experience on how to handle such situations, you will naturally feel safer and more confident. You will be able to withstand the discomfort and act accordingly to reestablish a state of safety.

2. Long-term integration and mastery. The more you resolve your old patterns and experiences, the less you get "*stuck in the past*". You will be able to enjoy life and deal with its regular ups and downs.

The first and most important action in a conflict is to move to a location that is safe. I believe that the further we have come in our healing process, the better we will be able to resist the urge to fall into old patterns of freeze or fawn reactions. The more we will be able to act according to our values, defend ourselves or flee - whatever is the most reasonable choice at hand. However, the actual fight/flight response is not the focus of the section. The assumption here is that you are already in a safe place, but might have just confronted a traumatic experience, e.g. through writing about what happened and what emotions you felt during and after the experience.

Use your observation to anchor yourself in the present. The traumatic experience is in the past. You are safe now. Take deep and slow breaths. Notice your breathing. Focus your awareness on body parts that are not filled with overwhelming emotions, like hands and feet. Look at your hands. Move them to make a fist and open your hands again. What do they feel like? Can you feel the blood flowing through them? What about your feet? Can you feel them? Look around you. Use your senses to anchor you in the present. Your experiences are long gone. What do you see? What colors can you see? Can you smell or hear anything? Even in the confined surroundings of an apartment, there can be five or more different noises at one time. The ventilation of your computer, electric appliances in the kitchen, rustling leaves, singing birds, pedestrians or cars on the street. In public places, you can easily identify 15 to 25 different sounds. Touch can also support you in this endeavor. What do your pants feel like? The rough surface of jeans can feel really nice and calming in this context. Social connection, physical touch and holding a conversation with someone who you feel comfortable around are also options to consider.

She snapped. Jumped away with a sudden, spiteful comment. The comment itself wasn't important. It wasn't bad; we weren't even arguing. Something about the situation just hit very close to home for some reason. I was shot out of reality. I started dissociating. All of a sudden, everything seems to be so... distant and blurry. The sidewalk, the cars, people playing basketball across the street. I freeze. I see her hand waving in front of my face, but I can't respond. She thinks I'm bullshitting, turns around and... walks away. What? What just happened? I feel trapped in a marble statue, unable to move or respond. It's like I just played red light, green light - and got stuck on a red light. Maybe I could move? But I really don't want to move right now. Tears start running down my face. I stand like this for a few minutes, before I finally start walking straight onwards. Where to? How? I don't know. Maybe she is waiting for me at the next corner? Just a little further. No one is here. I look around. Trees, a junction, a door. A huge, antique, wooden door.

It's more of a gate than a door. Only half of it seems to open for the local residents. I put my little scooter, Mirco, fourth of his name, on the doorstep in the half of the gate that I expect to stay closed and sit down. I start crying more intensely. Usually I like crying, it helps to resolve something and make me feel more relaxed. This... feels different. I cannot calm down. Is this a panic attack? I had read about them before. Either way - whatever it is, it isn't good. I have trouble slowing down my rapid, panic fueled breathing. Deep breaths, Fred. Slow and steady. No chance. My breath just keeps going at this frantic pace. My hands are feeling dizzy from the overload of oxygen in the muscles. They are cramping up, I can barely move them at all. I feel mute. I don't have the power to speak or cry out for attention. I am afraid of hyperventilating myself into unconsciousness. I'm alone in public in the dark. Not the best place to become unconscious. This is surreal. Fuck. I can only hope that someone passing will notice my state. There is an old lady in front of me, walking her dog. They both quickly realize that I need help. Nala, the dog, is an absolute lifesaver. She snuggles up to me and lets me pet her. I feel the texture of her fur on my hands. I focus on the texture. After a few minutes of this, I can start building more coherent sentences. I can even slow down my breathing a little, at least for a few moments. The sweet lady is patient and understanding with me. "That's okay, I'm not in a hurry" she says. I start holding small talk with her to distract myself from whatever this is. I ask about how she is doing and how her day has been. Bizarre. My hands are starting to slowly "unfreeze". Nala is so understanding. God bless her. The fur and the conversation are bringing me back to reality. It helps me to not spiral further down the rabbit hole I was losing myself in. I am sufficiently in control again to call a friend

*to pick me up and get me to safety. Phew. Maybe this is what they mean
when they say that recovery is a lifelong process[5] ?*

Expression of yourself leading to integration and mastery

Ok let's assume we have confronted an uncomfortable experience in writing. We expressed our anger and cried out about what happened. For intense trauma, the "immediate safety" is more important: to intuitively act out stored tension in the body, to anchor oneself in the present by observing the senses. For less intense situations, we might be inclined to let the dust settle and then simply go about our business. However, I like the thought of applying the restored fight-or-flight response to any challenging situation, as well as to our childhood patterns.

*When patients can physically experience what it would
have felt like to fight back or run away, they relax, smile
and express a sense of completion*

Bessel van der Kolk

Pierre Janet, the great pioneer in the research of trauma, whose thoughts are the foundation for several key ideas in this book, called it *"the pleasure of completed action"*. Recreating a successful response

---

5. Walker (2013): Complex PTSD

that would have helped us to overcome or flee from a dangerous situation creates this empowering sense of control over our life. So what can this response look like? And how do we practically apply it? For a successfully completed action it is important to imply a state of safety or that a fight or a flight has happened. Key elements to achieve this can include playfulness, movement, social connection and a safe environment. This means that several of the tools already discussed in earlier sections, like yoga, humor, or a solid posture and deep breaths, are applicable here. Anything that involves moving the body is wonderful as both fleeing and fighting involves a response from the body. Adding the element of self-expression is also beneficial. Consider the following:

- Singing

- dancing

- going for a walk

- running

- going to the gym

- any other sports

- gardening

- playing theatre

- making music

Creating an authentic flow from intuition to self-expression can be a blissful experience. The feeling of being heard or seen can also have a soothing effect, be it in conversations or through artistic expression like theater and music. Sometimes when I capture a disagreement in writing to resolve my feelings, I share my writings with the other person involved. Oftentimes, I don't even want to solve anything, to "win" or achieve any other outcome. It's just about being seen, heard and accepted in all my facets. To align my actions with my words, emotions and thoughts. Carrying out the listed activities in an isolated manner will also be beneficial for you. However, for effective trauma healing, it's crucial to have confronted the difficult experience right before the activity. For example, you could combine journaling with a subsequent run or visit to the gym.

Asserting boundaries to resolve anger and protect yourself

If a person actively does something to hurt you or cross your boundaries, you *always* have a choice. The mature response to reasonable, situational anger is to assert your boundaries. If your boundaries are crossed again, you can escalate the way you set your boundaries. If a friend speaks up in the group in a way that you don't like, sharing intimate stories about yourself; you can take them aside and tell them that you don't feel comfortable with private stories about yourself being shared. If it happens repeatedly and you don't feel like talking about it makes a difference, you can then escalate the way you set your boundary. You could question if you really want to keep such people as friends. If it happens repeatedly with different people, you could reconsider who you share your most intimate stories with. Technically, the moment you share something with someone, you give them the power to share it with others, even if you ask them not to. Have they sufficiently earned your trust in this regard yet? I feel like some people have a tendency to set boundaries too little too late and then be surprised if people walk all over them. You *always* have a choice or a way out! Just as much as you don't owe anything to anyone.

Anger is essential for this to work. If you are so accustomed to being treated badly or if you were taught to suppress anger, you might not even feel angry about being treated badly. You could be hurt, sad or confused, but the anger is either missing or blocked out. If this is the case, the work described in earlier chapters should be conducted first to awaken, feel and express anger. Redefining your values about how you should be treated will also help in letting a healthy anger come to life. It will indicate when you have been hurt or your boundaries have been crossed. It will empower you to look out for yourself and assert these boundaries. Having felt and expressed anger is also a prerequisite for forgiveness to take place; noting of course that some acts are so malicious that they can possibly never be forgiven. I like to think that seemingly contradicting truths can coexist: It's not ok what happened, but nonetheless I find empathy for aggressors and how they came to act the way they did.

Survivors need to resuscitate their instinctual anger about parental maltreatment or they risk blindly accepting others' reenactments of these behaviours

Pete Walker, Complex PTSD

If people are closer to you, they of course might deserve more chances than a stranger, or a new acquaintance. With a family member or partner it is probably reasonable to have more patience or put in more effort to improve things, to communicate and to set your boundaries before drastically limiting the power they have over your life, before you leave or push them out. However, even then you have no obligation to do anything. Let's say that you feel like your parents repeatedly treat you unfairly in one way or another as soon as you contact them. And you have made sure that your response to such situations has been reasonable, reflective and mature. Moreover, you feel like talking about your needs hasn't helped at all, possibly even led to arguments and ultimately made things worse. In this case, limit the contact to an intensity that is comfortable for you. You are allowed to do so!

Or imagine some guy is persisting on hitting on you and you feel obligated to talk to him, or to kiss him, or to take him home. Just because he was so nice or he bought you a drink or put in so much effort. You don't have to do anything if you're not comfortable with it, no matter what anyone else has told you or has done for you. You can *always* say no. Consent can *always* be taken away. Do you feel obligated to sleep with someone because you took them home, and now it would be silly to say no, even though you've now just started feeling uncomfortable? You start having pain during intercourse, but don't want to interrupt it? Speak up! It's okay to say no. It's important. A lot of people don't have the empathy or situational awareness to feel when you're uncomfortable. Maybe they even trust you to speak up and set boundaries if you're not comfortable?

> *Anyone can become angry - that is easy, but to be angry*
> *with the right person, to the right degree, at the right*
> *time,*
> *for the right purpose, and in the right way - this is not*
> *easy.*

Aristotle

Let's assume someone shouted at you at work. Maybe it was a supervisor so it would have been difficult to "talk back". And then at night, in meditation, you realize that they had no right to talk to you like that - and in hindsight you become angry. How dare they? The cool thing is that the better we become at this, the more we can protect ourselves in the present tense - and not just the day after. Imagine standing your ground firmly right away and being like: *"independent of my quality of work, you have no right to talk to me like that. Please watch your tone and your choice of words!"* and then leave the conversation. Ideally, the response will be in line with the level of "aggression". If someone is just slightly out of line or just in a funky mood and letting it out on me, I might tell them quietly that I respect them and their work, but this is generally not a work atmosphere I like working in. If someone is more aggressive, the assertion can also be more direct, ranging from the response shown above to even quitting my job. Everyone deserves an environment that treats them with respect.

It must be noted that some people act out their anger in rather harmful ways that hurt and damage others, often distracting themselves from emotions like sadness, fear or a feeling of unworthiness. In these cases the anger mostly blocks away the root emotion instead of helping to deal with your experiences. Think of a bully or a choleric, where anger and a hot temper are more of a regular pattern than a direct response to someone actually attacking them.

Also, I recommend to focus on resolving the emotion with the techniques described in this book, but do not make decisions in this state of being! Wait till some time has passed and you have cooled down, before making any decisions that might have a larger impact on your life. Sometimes, a good night's sleep will rectify the situation more than one could expect in the heat of the moment.

Chapter Nine

The Christmas incident

The following story will hopefully bring to life several principles that have already been discussed throughout this part of the book:

- Abuse doesn't always have to be physical, or even verbal

- How to set and escalate boundaries

- How to establish an immediate sense of safety

- How to re-confront and resolve traumatic experiences

- The power of social connection and belonging

It is a (slightly modified and shortened) excerpt from a letter that I wrote to my mom about two days after the incident that took place on the 23rd of December during the reign of Mirco the third.

Briefly about my condition: I was fine. I was well rested. I was calm. I read a lot on the train. Things are going well at work. I cooked myself something for the journey. I was in a rock solid, healthy, loving state. I was happy to see you. I love you.

We just had a short, heated discussion in the living room. When I - admittedly in an agitated manner - asked you to be more appreciative of me playing the piano, you just responded with "Don't be such a sensitive little boy". A phrase you like to use when I try to establish a more appreciative way of communicating. You are telling me to just put up with things that bother and hurt me. You are denying the legitimacy of my set boundaries and feelings and their right to exist. That is not okay. That pisses me off. I have the right to ask for respectful behavior. We can talk about what that looks like in detail. Maybe I am overreacting or asking for too much. Maybe I am sensitive in this regard. Maybe we will just conclude that we have different points of view and see things differently. But to dismiss my request as baseless from the outset is not okay. You went on to look for and name reasons why I might be so irritable, suggesting that there was something wrong with me. There is nothing wrong with me. I am a healthy, mature and reflected adult. If I set a boundary, then I'm all of a sudden "sick, irritable and overloaded". What the hell?

Now I'm in my room and angry. Why did I get angry this quickly? You obviously hit a soft spot with your comment. I want to sort myself out, observe the anger and reflect on what has just happened. You come to the door and talk to me. I am dismissive. I am cynical. I am grateful to you for making me dinner. However, I don't show this gratitude because I'm angry about what happened in the living room. I ask you to leave. The first time I say coldly, "Go!". The second time I say pleadingly, "Please go!". In total, I ask you to leave about 8 to 12 times. I don't want to talk to you at this moment. I want to sort myself out, observe the anger and reflect on what just happened. You are ignoring my boundary and crossing it. I keep escalating the way I set my boundary and you keep ignoring it time and time again. How can you be so ignorant of my needs? I wanted nothing from you. I just wanted my space. My space. My life. My peace. Me. "Retreat!" I shout. I scream. I plead. I even announce that I'm about to come out and will physically remove you if you don't leave soon. You continue to ignore my requests. I go out and yell at you to leave and still you refuse. [Note: at this point I physically grab my mom and push her to the end of the hallway into her room, about 10 meters away. She did not get hurt]. My physical assault was not intended to cause harm at any time. It was a controlled expression of anger for the sole purpose of removing you from my space. Self-protection. Self-determination. Me.

The next time we cross paths in the house you comment on my "lack of emotional control" and "uncontrolled outburst of rage" and - once again - you deny my feelings and their right to exist. My anger and escalation was an important and healthy mechanism to set my boundary and to see what is good for me. Without that aggression, I would have continued to talk to you, even though at that moment I really wanted to be alone.

If you seek me out in my safe space, invade it with your immediate need for conversing, and ignore my countless requests to respect my place of retreat, then I no longer have a place of retreat in this house. I have no place where I can be alone, reflect, feel safe. The feeling of a safe environment is essential for the self to come to terms with the end of a dangerous situation or conflict situation, to reflect, to classify and to heal. I feel attacked at the core of my being and not accepted or respected. I have no place where I can process these feelings in peace and safety. The only way out as a healthy, self-respecting adult is to leave. I feel a knot in my chest at the thought of returning to the house or you today or tomorrow. I do not feel safe.

Now for the last part - in your bedroom. I came to you. I worked through my anger and came to you in a loving, safe, constructive state.

I want to leave on good terms. I want to thank you for the food. I want to give you a hug. I understand that you are hurt and disappointed. I understand that you don't understand - how could you, you treat me the same way you always have. I like to comfort you and hold you. I love you. I am frightened by the size and strength of the demons that accompany you and attack you. But: I cannot leave without a legitimate fear of your suicide. Against my own needs (again, they are ignored and violated) you ask me to stay so that I protect you from yourself.

Yet you explicitly threaten me with my own feelings of how I would feel if I left and you killed yourself. This is blatant, gross, psychological violence. I cannot and will not express it in any other way. What a blow. What incredible aggression, hurt and pain. I no longer feel safe in your presence. You are my mother and I want us to have a good relationship. As much as I would want to and as much as I like you: I cannot come back and visit you right now because I have no reason to rule out a repeat of this stark, traumatic experience. My body alone switches to danger and stress at the thought. Also: You care more about what other people think about us than what is good for me. "What are people supposed to think if you leave now, right before Christmas?" you asked me. There is no reason to feel ashamed. It's okay to argue. It's okay to set my boundaries and find my space elsewhere.

Victims of trauma can quickly be overwhelmed by sudden changes in environment. An old friend of mine once cut open her arms and legs when her best friend unexpectedly ended their friendship. Even though I am 100% sure that I need to leave, I still have to take my mom's threat

seriously. I want to make things as smooth as possible for her. I briefly inform my brother about the situation and get him to call my mom, while I get ready and pack my things. Once I see that she is on the phone with him, I leave. Transitioning from "being together" to "being on the phone" to "being alone" is easier for her than transitioning from "being together" to all of a sudden "being alone". It will lower the chances of any self-harm taking place. At this point it is around 10pm and I've found a friend who lives about one and a half hours away by train who is willing to take me in for Christmas. God bless him.

It is about 3° Celsius outside and snowing lightly. The train station is roughly 11km away from home. Luckily, my old inline skates still do the trick. Skating away from this situation was the best I could do. I am responsible for my safety. I am able to flee. I am able to set boundaries and defend them, no matter the circumstances. There is also utter pain and sadness about what happened, about not spending Christmas at home and about the state of my relationship with my mom. It's okay. I will be okay.

The family I stayed with was marvelous. They sincerely welcomed me, they got last-second Christmas gifts for me and they showed interest in me - without asking uncomfortable questions about what happened. I felt seen and accepted, and most importantly - I felt safe. Safe enough to write a 5,000 word, 10 page letter to my mom about what happened, about my childhood and emotions that had never been put into words before. I found it greatly soothing and healing to voice my feelings about my childhood losses and injustices. Once back home in Vienna, I went to see my old therapist for a session to reflect on my behavior. I wanted to find out if I could have acted any differently and to ask what else I could do to heal from the incident.

In the aftermath, I was scared to go out for a few days. I didn't feel safe in public for another three to four weeks, especially in more crowded *places like inner city supermarkets. Sometimes it takes a while for the dust to settle. Other than that, I recovered surprisingly well. I am mostly proud of the way I behaved, though my anger was quite quick to arise in response to criticism; it seems like there is still a defense mechanism that I might want to uncover at some point. Sometimes I have trouble accepting imperfection or dealing with criticism. That's okay. I feel like everything I've been working on for years makes sense. I apparently knew how to confront and overcome extremely difficult situations and emotions. The letter was a big step towards a better relationship with my mom (at least for me, maybe not so much for her). But I feel like she has been more respectful of my boundaries ever since. Also, I have no hidden resentments left about the past and I visit her regularly. Sometimes things have to escalate before they can calm down again. I love you mom.*

Rewriting the story - what would affection and safety have looked like?

With the last part, we wanted to achieve a combination of trauma-confrontation and subsequent expression that simulates a successful fight-or-flight response to the brain in order to resolve the experience. We are creating a new storyline where we (re-)confront the traumatic experience, e.g. in writing, and then successfully fight it or flee from it through sports or other forms of self-expression. In the original situation this fight/flight response probably never happened. Luckily, the brain doesn't care about that. It can't even properly distinguish between imagination and memory[1]. It just wants to get over the past. How we achieve that is not of importance, as long as we do achieve it.

Bessel van der Kolk uses the example of five-year-old Noam, a witness of the 9/11 incidents. Noam adds trampolines to his drawing of people jumping out of the burning towers so that *"next time when people have to jump, they will be safe"*. He imagined a more positive alternative to what he had witnessed. Van der Kolk also talks about family constellations, where patients would imagine an ideal version of their parents and families with all the affection, love and support that they would have wished for. I myself have successfully used this in several therapy sessions. What would an ideal childhood have looked like? How would teachers, peers, and family have behaved differently? What would a present, positive father figure have looked like for me? How can I give these qualities to myself? The same line of questions can also apply to situations where I didn't fully stand up for myself or that I am not happy with. In a more positive scenario, what could I have said? What could I have done differently? How could I have defended myself better? Once acceptance and acknowledgement for something dreadful has been established, reimagining the line of events in a more positive way is a wonderful feel-good way of capacity building and healing.

---

1. See Maltz (1960): Psycho-Cybernetics

"*Wunderkind*" Barbara said, with that soft, angelic voice and that gorgeous smile of hers. I wasn't entirely sure if she was a muse, a friend or a partner. How bold though! How dare she? She knew my story. I was eight years old when I entered the next level of school. Children are usually ten or eleven at this point. Word about my skills in mental arithmetic and drawing square roots had quickly spread throughout the entire school. I was put on this pedestal as some form of wonder child. Oftentimes, students had heard of the "*Wunderkind*" even before they heard my actual name. People in the hallways would stop me just to ask mathematical questions like "24 times 17? Quick!" Half the time they couldn't even check the results of their questions, as mobile phones weren't in fashion yet. It's 408 by the way, in case you were starting to wonder. I felt like a slot machine - pay with a minute of your time and get to see the newest hyperbrain in action.

Paired with my somewhat limited social skills at the time, this made for an overall unpleasant experience. It didn't take long for the class bullies to pick up the word and use it for mockery and insults. "*Wunderkind*" was, for me, representative of how socially excluded I had been, and how little I was seen for who I actually was - just a kid. No surprise that I developed a strong dislike for the word. I really didn't want to be called "*Wunderkind*" and I really didn't want to think of that past. She didn't care about any of that. Or maybe she did - and knew that her affection would be able to transcend all of that. At first I wanted to protest. But how could I possibly protest such bold and sweet affection? She took something that was used to hurt me and bully me and turned it into something wonderful and affectionate. It was too disarming to say anything - and she persisted in using that name every now and then anyways. It reminded me that, despite the pain these characteristics might've brought with them back then, they are now a part of my identity that helps me in advancing my career, or in compiling complex ideas *(more or less) concisely, like in this book. It nurtured humility and resolved pain. She rewrote a part of my story and I am most grateful for that.*

Short outlook on other tools

There are a couple of tools and aspects that have crossed my path in only minor ways. I am generally aware of their potential benefits, but don't feel comfortable going into too much detail. I shall therefore simply name them and quickly describe them here, so that you are aware of their existence.

Social connection - a lot of the principles discussed in this book focus on oneself. I also want to highlight the importance of social connections for healing and resilience. The feeling of belonging to a group, moving in synchronicity with a group or a stable relationship with someone who you feel safe with, can all be important elements on the journey to a compassionate and capable way of life. The responsibility you might carry as part of your role in a club (be it sports, music, or another hobby) can fill your life with meaning. It can give you the feeling of being seen, accepted and capable. Social relationships don't even have to be with other humans; the non-questioning nature of animals like horses, dogs or cats can sometimes be even more beneficial than humans. Your horse is (hopefully) not going to ask you how you feel about your childhood, your parents, or your day, while your therapist just might. Your horse will just be there for you.

In a social context it's helpful to develop some sort of semi-permeability: a concept used in biology to describe membranes that only let some materials pass through. In this context it's about understanding which influences to block from entering your life, and which ones to allow. Stop allowing behavior that puts you down, but don't let that stop you from opening up in relationships.

EMDR - Eye movement desensitization and reprocessing. This is a very effective method of therapy for healing and resolving one-time traumatic incidents. It is potentially also effective with traumatic patterns established over a longer period of time.

IFS - Inner family systems therapy. Based on the theory that everyone acts out different roles, like child, critic or protector. This type of therapy is oriented towards identifying, accepting and integrating these roles and aspects of yourself.

Neurofeedback uses computers that measure your brainwaves to teach you how to reach states of low arousal and high relaxation. It can be a very effective way to start healing without engaging in verbal interaction or cognitive behavioral therapy.

Psychopharmaceuticals and their benefits are highly disputed in the scientific community.[2] Let's take depression as an example to have a closer look. Depression is linked to childhood trauma, especially neglect and emotional abuse. This plays into the ideas laid out in this book: experiences are too challenging to be resolved right away, they get stuck in the present and are necessarily blocked to enable the patient to keep living a normal life. By resisting the flow of experience,

---

2. For the following statements, see for example:Lacasse, Leo (2005): Serotonin and Depression: A Disconnect between the Advertisements and the Scientific Literature Cowen, Browning (2015): What has serotonin to do with depression? Mandelli, Petrelli, Serretti (2015): The role of specific early trauma in adult depression: A meta-analysis of published literature. Childhood trauma and adult depression

positive aspects of life are equally suppressed - leading to a grey and depressed perception of life.

Since the 80s, the belief that depression is instead linked to lower serotonin levels was pushed by the pharmaceutical industry, especially in the United States. In the US, it is allowed to directly advertise pharmaceutical drugs to consumers, causing an obvious conflict of interest. Antidepressants are supposed to fix a supposed "chemical imbalance" in the brain by increasing these serotonin levels. However, there is no scientific consensus confirming this view. Studies often have methodological flaws, small sample sizes or the drugs barely out-perform the placebos. Nonetheless, antidepressants have been shown to be rather helpful for some patients. They can help teach the brain to process emotional information in a more positive way. They can also promote establishing new behavior by increasing the speed of building new connections in the brain.

Chapter Ten

A sense of identity

A dream was born

What is freedom? Are we ever truly free? Antoine Girard certainly seemed like he was free. He starred in a cineastic short film documentary, where he worked on breaking the height record in paragliding. There he was, in the Himalayas, soaring through the crisp mountain air with just a couple of strings and two oversized plastic bags as his aid. One above his head to fly and the other connected to the strings, holding his body in place. The wind whistled through the strings, and the world below looked like a miniature model. He had thousands of meters of space all around him. I don't think anything comes as close to the human dream of flight as paragliding does. Certainly more than commercial flights which to me don't feel that different to your standard ride on the subway. In paragliding, it's really just you. Up there, with the hawks. No gravity, no one to bother you, no deadline creeping up on you. To me, that is freedom.

I watched this documentary at the time of the reign of Mirco the third, my scooter and steady companion at the time. I was somewhere in my early-mid twenties, in the middle of my master's degree, something related to sustainability. So far, I had mostly been drifting about like an astronaut in space that had lost connection to his ship - without a clear purpose or path. I might have stopped ending up at a club four nights a week and bored on the computer the other three. The newly established habits of working and studying however were mostly owed to some strange sense of duty. I didn't know this at the time, but sustainability had mostly been an excuse not to have to get to know myself. I mean, even if I was wrong, who's going to be like... "Oh man, you really wasted those years trying to save the planet"? If I didn't know who I was, the least I could do was to analytically maximize my objective benefit for society and the planet.

Watching Antoine Girard glide through the Himalayan sky is when it hit me. I could do whatever the hell I wanted with my body, my time, my life. I could actively think about what I would like to do. Who I wanted to be. What would be fun for me. This guy thought it would be fun to fly around the highest mountains on earth. To go hiking and flying in the Pakistani mountains, not knowing if the local rebels would let him keep his life. He was truly treating the world as his playground. Others in the same set of short films thought it would be fun to Rollerski from the North of Canada to the border of Mexico, to go mountain biking north of the polar circle or to freeride the slopes of Mont Blanc.

I didn't quite manage to apply this mindset to my vocation just yet. In the domain of money making, I preferred sticking to my narrow-minded set of beliefs for now: degree, employment, stability. For hobbies however, I started to be more daring. And truer to myself. I wanted to fly. Maybe not breaking records, and maybe not in the Himalayas, but certainly up there. My sense of adventure was awakened. I wanted to be as free as Antoine Girard was. I was excited for what the future held.

Building a strong sense of identity

The definition of self-esteem brought up earlier can be summarized with "*I am worthy of good*" and "*I am capable of good*". To successfully achieve both, the concept one has of oneself is crucial. How can I be convinced of my capabilities of good, if I don't understand who I am, what I can do or where I am supposed to go? How can I be convinced of my "deserving of goodness" when I don't know who I am? So... who am I? What do I associate with the concept of "I"? What is my identity? What (or who) do I identify with?

The German Wikipedia states that identity "*...is the collection of particularities that characterize an entity [..] and distinguish it as an individual from others*". This includes all of the things we relate to - be it in a good or bad way. An interplay of differentiation and belonging.

Imitation is one of the key principles of how we as humans develop ourselves. This is why role models are so important when growing up.[1] Who are your role models? Kids can develop and build their own sense of identity from the characteristics of role models combined with their own experiences. In order to gain a better understanding of our identity now, we can ask ourselves an endless set of questions; the following are just a few examples. Feel free to come up with more of them on your own. All of them are in one way or another about how you relate to the world:

- What do I like and dislike?

- What are my strengths and weaknesses?

- What do my friends value me for? (if you don't know, go ask them)

- What are my ethical and moral standards?

- What groups, clubs, social circles, regions do I feel like I belong to?

- What are my emotional habits?

- What were my most defining childhood moments and patterns?

- Which values are uncompromisable for me?

- What am I doing when I am having fun?

---

1. Daum, Gampe (2016): Psychologie und Erziehung: Die Rolle von Vorbildern in der sozial-kognitiven Entwicklung. See also: Vygotsky (1978): Mind and society: The development of higher psychological processes; Marcia (1980): Identity in adolescence

- How do I treat my fellow human beings?

- How do I treat myself?

- How do I *want to* treat myself and others?

- What are the people around me spending their time with?

- Who are my idols?

- Which needs of mine are currently met and unmet?

- Who do I want to be?

- What do I want to do?

It is important to proceed here without any judgement whatsoever. It is merely about observing and acknowledging what is there. Crucial for success is the overcoming of repression of thoughts, emotions and feelings. If you like wearing socks with sandals, that's okay. Knowing our emotional patterns and habits helps us to accept all aspects of our experiences and therefore to accept ourselves. In a wider sense, our bodies, our thoughts and our emotions are also just experiences and perceptions.

Finding responses to the list of questions above, or at least spending time with them, also goes hand in hand with understanding the path ahead of you - your visions and long-term goals. Once you are more aware of yourself and more knowledgeable about yourself, you can "simply" align your main goals with your identity, your preferences and your values. A lack of connection to emotions, beliefs or values is often associated with a general lack of self-awareness and self-knowledge. This can lead to people mightily struggling with choosing career paths or hobbies until they start working on their sense of identity. It also makes plenty of smaller decisions much easier; you don't have to think every time you want to do something, you can just check if it is aligned with your set of values and preferences.

A man's values are the product of the thinking he has done or failed to do

Nathaniel Branden[2]

After reading the sections about trauma, bonding and relationships, you might come to question this sudden responsibility. After all, the sections clearly elaborate the impact of early childhood experiences on who you are today. And yes, childhood and parents had an influence on your set of values and self-concept and all that. But what you do from here onwards is up to you. Personalities aren't set in stone, they are fluid. Isn't that exciting? Your past may serve as an explanation of how you got here, but it can never serve as an excuse for not pulling yourself together from now on[3]. Actually, it is the complete opposite: now that you have (hopefully) gotten insights as to why things are the way they are, you have no excuse not to change them. You are accountable for what you do from now on! You know what? Actually I will personally hold you accountable. Once you have read the whole book and maybe some time has passed - feel free to write to me at fred.pantarhei@gmail.com and tell me how things are

---

2. Branden (1969): The Psychology of Self-Esteem

3. See Farrelly, Brandsma (1981): Provocative Therapy; Branden (1974): The Disowned Self

going. What are you struggling with? What have you achieved and accomplished? How are you feeling?

Everyone is capable of (re-)defining and identifying their values. We are all capable of making different choices and creating different habits. As humans, we are given the incredible ability to witness, reason and adapt both our behavior and actions. I think it's even our duty as humans to do so - our responsibility of reason. We have evolved beyond the harmony of the animal kingdom, which is blindly in unison with nature. We cannot just be guided by animalistic behavioral patterns or instinctive impulses. We cannot just suspend our ability to reason. Not defining these values consciously and not recognizing the "necessity of thought", as Branden puts it, is still a twisted expression of consciousness. In his eyes, a revolt against the *"responsibility of reason and thought"* includes a revolt against the *"responsibility of self-awareness"*, the necessity of which we have hopefully laid out sufficiently so far.

A strong sense of identity - Owning the disowned self

Everyone has the potential for darkness. Take a moment to ask yourself: might you have been a Nazi? And of course your impulse is going to be "What? Me? Noooo...". But think about it for a second. You have been observing political developments with worry for some time but now it's too late to speak up or start a public protest. You can either live in safety and supposed ignorance, and potentially even benefit financially; or you can risk the lives of you and your entire family, "just" because of some sense of righteousness or to help a few strangers from the village. What would you do? From this perspective, it seems impossible to value the bravery of resistance movements at the time of the Third Reich.

The actions of Nazis were monstrous and inhumane and the horrors conducted were of unimaginable sorts. But Nazis themselves - at the end of the day, they were still humans, despite all the atrocities committed. There was just a very specific set of variables in society tweaked in a way that allowed and enabled this darkness to rise. We dehumanize people that do terrible things (*"what a monster"*), not realizing that these aspects are potentially dormant in mankind in general. I think it's crucial to think about these things and accept them to a certain degree to keep them in check. Let's look at examples that are more relatable to your current life:

We tend to "disown[4] parts of our lives that we perceive as being unacceptable or shameful, like desires, emotions, personality traits, aspects of our physical appearance, or beliefs and values. Let's say someone has grown up in a conservative Christian fashion and has been faithful to their partner, but then meets someone else that awakens their desires. Or they might have the fleeting wish of attacking someone. But since "they would never do such a thing" there is no point in wondering about any denial in the first place. And so the desire or the wish remains, however not accepted as part of the self. Where can we meet aspects that remain in life but that we don't consider to be a part of ourselves? Obviously outside of us - in the world, in others![5] Suddenly, others appear to be angry or show signs of the desires suppressed in the self.

---

4. C.f. Branden (1972): The Disowned Self

5. Wilber (1979): No Boundary, p. 87ff

We end up with a distorted view of the self, suppressed emotions that don't get to be resolved - and people bringing facets into our own life that we really don't understand as there is no apparent reason for such behavior. This makes it all the more important to integrate all facets of ourselves and accept them, as uncomfortable as they may be. Whenever I meet people that know how to push my buttons, I ask myself: *what aspect about them do I not like? Is there any chance that I have the same feature, behavior or characteristic without being aware of it?* I like the idea that even the most annoying people can be wonderful mirrors and support me in my journey of self-discovery. And the further one moves in this process of self-integration, the more difficult it becomes for other people to push any buttons. After all - everything about you that they can play around with, you already faced and accepted a long time ago.

A strong sense of identity - knowing what is within your power

Let's look at the understanding of what is within our power. Being able to differentiate between the aspects of a challenge that are under your control and not under your control is incredibly important. It's necessary to understand that we *can* do something about a problem in order to unlock the full potential for solving the problem. On the other hand, not understanding that something is *outside* of our control just leads to needless suffering and burning energy. For example, whether someone responds to your message or not is in *their* control, not yours. If that frustrates you, then you have a goal (to get a response) in someone else's area of control - and are subsequently dependent on other people acting to your liking. This is bound to lead to frustration or suffering sooner or later, as long as you still have expectations in the "area of control" of other people. What *is* ok however, is to *generally* expect people to respond to you in a timely manner. If that's something that is important to you personally, you could specifically look for people in your life that always respond quickly and exclude people that don't. Who you *don't* keep around is in *your* control; who you *do* keep around is of course again dependent on the consent of the other person in the matter. I personally think there are more important values to look for in friends and partners than their response time to messages, like how funny they are, how they treat me or how I feel around them. The well-known serenity prayer also summarizes this whole concept quite nicely:

God, grant me the serenity to accept the things I cannot change,
Courage to change the things I can,
And wisdom to know the difference.

Reinhold Niebuhr

Let's breathe some more life into this with another example:

I got deducted a grade on my thesis for "choosing the wrong topic". This was despite the fact that I had thoroughly discussed the topic choice with my counsellor at the beginning of the seminar. I felt like I was being treated unfairly. So, what is in my area of influence here? I could go into the counsellor's office and urinate on his carpet while holding eye contact, just to show dominance and demonstrate my appreciation for rebellion. That would, however, most likely not improve my situation and probably lead to criminal charges being pressed. I ended up settling for sending him an email in which I referred to the university guidelines for judging theses. I never got a response. By the time I realized that I would never get a response, a couple of weeks had passed and my grade was put into the system, meaning that it could no longer be changed. I was convinced that he *should* not have downgraded me for such a silly reason. I was angry. Writing about my anger or voicing it somehow to resolve the emotion was important. But I could have also taken several further steps after sending my mail. I could have called. I could have personally gone to his office and demanded a face-to-face explanation. I could have escalated to his secretary, to the principal or to other governance boards at university. Only if all of those steps had failed, would it have been about accepting the outcome. Since I didn't realize the possibilities in my influence soon enough, I couldn't unlock the full potential of solving the problem and subsequently I had to bear some of the responsibility for the outcome. Realizing this makes it much easier for me to not spiral into a whiny mode of "*he should have done this, the university should have done that*".

A strong sense of identity - the benefits of decision making

The habit of proactively making decisions will improve your quality of life. I am calling this a habit because I think that you can actively work on it. Decision making for me is similar to courage. You do not *have* courage, you *do* courage. You *decide* to act courageously in a situation and jump over your shadow. Ideally you build a habit of ignoring the limits of your comfort zone. Similarly, I think you can build a habit of making decisions in a more straightforward manner and benefit from the results of less hesitation, regret or stagnation.

A decision will change some aspect of your life. Ideally, the initiated change will improve your situation in some form. For example, the simple act of deciding to cook some food will hopefully put an end to you feeling hungry. And if you end up with a worst-case scenario, then you have learned a valuable lesson on how to better improve your situation in the future. If it turns out that your cooking is bad, then next time you might just order takeout instead. Or you might make the time to learn more about cooking before your next attempt. Or, if your peers gave you a hard time about your decision to wear socks with sandals, you might end up putting on actual shoes next time. Either way, some form of development and improvement will certainly take place, be it a lesson or a change for the better.

I'm not a big fan of the so-called "once in a lifetime opportunities" that you *have* to take and supposedly can not decide against, be it for business, jobs or partners. It only artificially inflates the value of something you have because you look at it from a perspective of scarcity. Life usually runs in patterns and what happened once is very likely to happen again. Especially when the problems aren't... that big or prominent. If your boss or your partner are physically abusive, you have a strong incentive to do something about your situation. However, if they are just... not a good fit, or merely mediocre, then you lack a strong incentive to change something. This is where being eager to make decisions will come in handy.

There are a few aspects to choice and decision making that are rather counterintuitive.[6] Having too many options for a choice generally leads to more regret and less satisfaction. It mostly feels overwhelming, having to evaluate all the options and then trying to identify the one that is supposedly the best. Anything above 6 options will lead to more worry about making the right decision and less satisfaction about the actual outcome. For example, I would not recommend dating more than 6 people at once before choosing a partner as it just leads to complications.

Restrict your degrees of freedom when making decisions

Go have a look at Jack Butcher's *Visualize Value*. He uses very minimalistic white on black graphs to convey his messages. This enables him to focus his effort on the highest point of contribution - the idea and the content of his image. It also saves him the effort of making countless decisions around color, content or illustration every time he creates an image[7] . Similarly, as a vegan, choosing a plate when going out for dinner is a simple process. I just take the one meal on the menu that is vegan. If there are two or three, I focus on protein or personal preference. Ta-da - choice made. No regret about opportunity costs or

---

6. Check out Schwartz (2004):"The Paradox of Choice: Why More Is Less" for a very interesting read on this topic

7. Credits to Chris Williamson's Podcast "Modern Wisdom" where he talks about this

potentially different outcomes. To be honest, I would find the thought of people turning vegan simply for this reason rather entertaining. Anyways. We live in a world where we are constantly bombarded with too much input, be it information, colors, noise, advertisements and possibilities. I think it's become necessary to artificially restrict your "degrees of freedom" when making choices in a way that decreases paralysis or worry before making the decision and significantly increasing subsequent satisfaction.

Stop overestimating the impact of decisions

In 2003, Wilson and Gilbert introduced the concept of affective forecasting in a rather interesting study[8]. Affective forecasting refers to people's ability - or lack thereof - to accurately predict their future emotional states. The authors argue that people often have difficulties with affective forecasting due to certain factors that are rather common:

Firstly, people fail to "...*anticipate how much their psychological immune systems will hasten their recovery*". They call this phenomenon *immune neglect*. In other words, we easily forget about our own resilience in dealing with negative experiences. Secondly, people tend to focus solely on the event in question and ignore other factors that may influence their emotional state. This can lead to an overestimation of the impact of the event on their overall well-being. If we become aware of this two-fold bias in overestimating the potential negative impacts of decisions, we can hopefully make decisions with more ease and

---

8. Wilson, Gilbert (2003): Affective Forecasting

less worry about the outcome. Sometimes when I have trouble with a decision, I ask myself how I might feel about this decision 5 years into the future looking back. This resolves any worries rather quickly as I will most likely have forgotten about most of the decisions anyway.

Go for what is good enough, not for what is best

It is not always feasible or pragmatic to somehow reduce the number of options we have when making a choice. I am aware that this is a bit of a first world problem, but bear with me here: Imagine you don't have to worry about cost of living and are looking for a place to study after high school. Artificially restricting yourself to one random state or country simply to limit your options wouldn't do you much good in this case, would it? In cases like these, I like to simply identify an option that fits my predefined set of criteria, instead of having to evaluate *all* the options available on the market. To go for what is good enough, not for what is best. Surprisingly, this idea of "good enough" helps with bigger decisions (job, partner, place to live etc.) even more than with smaller decisions (what to wear on your night out or what to have for dinner). It also supports acceptance of your choice in the aftermath. Sticking to this will prevent you from constantly worrying if there might have been a better choice. If there might be a better partner out there, or a better university, or a better place to live. You will be less inclined to fall victim to these worries if you picked one that is simply good enough for you. Though, of course, I hope that your criteria for a "good enough partner" are slightly more demanding than your criteria for a "good enough lunch".

Focus on structural decision making & compound effects

This idea alone is worth exploring in several different books as it borderlines the topics of habit building, the compound effect of incremental change and the nature of neurological pathways[9] . For now, I just want to make an appeal for focusing decision making on structural parts of your life. To shift your criteria for decision making from impulse to alignment with your long-term path and vision. If you have spent time on deciding what you want or what you want to want, or what kind of person you want to be, most decisions in life will simply be a check against your values and goals. If you have a clear understanding of how you structurally want to balance playfulness and work in your life, there should be no issue in prioritizing all the different options on a free Saturday. If you are aware of your desired balance between indulgence and long-term health in terms of what you consume, then you won't have to decide what's for dinner based on your impulses on a random Thursday night.

Don't practise what you do not want to become

Jordan Peterson[10]

---

9. See for example James Clear (2018): Atomic Habits, Jordan Peterson's Maps of Meaning lectures or the chapters "Addiction" and "Rewiring the brain - being patient with our progress"

10. In one of his lectures

The thing is, the brain's rapid way of building new pathways is both a blessing and a curse. Every time you do something, your state and your surroundings are linked to that specific action. Every time you do that same thing again, the link is strengthened. The next time you find yourself in a similar state or surrounding, you are more likely to pursue the same course of action. There is no need to focus on big, sudden changes in life. Our basic, daily habits around food, sleep, rest, movement, education, free time and drugs determine most of who we are. Over time, these tiny actions compound rather quickly to make up who we are, so don't practice what you don't want to become.

Chapter Eleven

Know thyself?

A *bit more than a year had passed since my watching of Girard's documentary. The reign of Mirco the third had come to a sudden stop. One day, while driving down a central Viennese road to work, I suddenly had the steering bar in my hands - without any connection left to the board. The board itself went on to roll into oncoming traffic before crashing into the opposite sidewalk. That's what happens when you stop steering. Hehe. Anyways. I had finished my master's degree. I had somehow managed to find a job and an apartment. Moreover, I had even managed to financially stay afloat through the summer, before the job actually started in October.*

Now what? The pride of graduating soon gave way to a feeling of emptiness. No more student clubs, no university field trips, no side jobs that were mostly based on events and social interaction. Also no deadlines to adhere to, no thesis to write and no exam to study for. After work, I would go home and stare at the wall until the rest of the evening had passed. Was this what my life would be like from now on? One evening, I pulled out an old vision board that I had started about a year before. At the top, arrows were leading away from the word "THINK" written in blue crayon in the top-left corner to the word "ACT" written in red in the top-right corner. My name, Fred, was written in the center connecting to themes around it. In one of these themes on the left, I had started collecting my "superheroes". I had come across the idea of imagining a team of "superheroes" standing behind you in difficult situations and supporting you. I really liked the idea for presenting in front of large crowds, as it made the stage feel more powerful and less empty compared to the audience. Think of grandma whispering a snarky comment in your ear while you wait to begin your speech. So far, my superheroes consisted of characters I had come across in series and films that showed some overlap with my values or goals. Like Harvey Specter from Suits ("It's going to happen, because I'm going to make it happen"), Louise from Bob's Burgers with her enthusiasm for chaos ("Don't tell me to shut up") or Ygritte from Game of Thrones ("You know nothing, Fred Snow"). Underneath, I had written my values in the color that I thought was most corresponding to each value, like acceptance and outcome in-dependence in a dark blue, humility and empathy in a forest green or loyalty in purple. The remaining values were love, gratitude, forgiveness, and self-respect. There are likely more superheroes and values that are important to me, but I assume I just never actually finished the exercise. You know how it goes.

After getting lost in reminiscing about these values and heroes, and about the last time I had touched my vision board, I started to collect my thoughts. This time, my focus was more about doing rather than being. Actions, rather than values. There were bits and pieces of hobbies and preferences here and there, but nothing structured. What do I like? Who do I want to be? I started with listing six core needs (physical, sexual, spiritual, intellectual, social and emotional) and assessed my current level of fulfillment in these categories. Behind "emotional", I had to put a question mark. I might have gone to therapy and roughly learned how to deal with shit, but I still don't think that I was really feeling myself.

As a second task, I freely listed words that came to mind when I thought about myself 5-10 years into the future. Words like "free spirit", "well dressed" or "impact" came to mind. My third list consisted of hobbies, activities and interests that had brought me joy in the past or that I might want to cultivate in the future. Theater, psychology, spirituality, piano, paragliding, writing, photography and racing.

The three that spoke to me the most were piano, paragliding and psychology. I had been playing the piano for around two and a half years at this point, I was proud of my progress, and it was a great teacher in withstanding short-term frustration in exchange for long-term gratification. Whenever I wanted to spend time doing something joyful, I would just sit down and play the pieces I could play by heart for half an hour. There was something magical about playing pieces by heart. At some point, the muscle memory becomes so engraved in the fingers that you don't have to consciously think about what you have to do anymore. The piece just plays itself. This enabled me to lose myself in a way - while still being me. It's like there was no pianist and no piano. The only thing left was the process of playing the piano. The process of the music coming to life. I was the music, not the pianist.

Now that I was earning money above the poverty line, I was in a position of being able to afford the license and equipment required for paragliding with reasonable saving efforts. And about psychology (and spirituality)... well it had always been an interest of mine. It began at the age of 8 when I was three years younger than everyone else around me, and I wondered how I could possibly cross such a bridge. It continued when I started reading spiritual and philosophical texts at the age of 15 and it certainly became important when I was somewhat overwhelmed by my relationship experiences in my twenties.

Subsequently, I created what I like to call "actionable mind maps". They would cover any possible aspects and steps related to the hobby. This ranged from concrete, applicable next steps, to collecting surrounding thoughts to envisioning how I might be practicing the activity ten years down the line. My piano mind map for example included potential genres to move into, influential composers, and thoughts around publishing, composing and building a music-related network. An important piece of the puzzle in these maps was the gut feeling that came in the following weeks (or even years). To conjure sufficient courage to continue when something is uncomfortable requires the passion of chasing a dream (or lots and lots of discipline). It requires the certainty that you are doing what you are supposed to do. And for me and piano... well... that wasn't it. I like it, but at the end of the day, it's just a hobby. I might have learned a new piece or played here and there, and I still plan on composing something further down the line. Playing all-time favorites like the Liszt arrangement of Danse Macabre is also still on my bucket list. But to this day, I have never published any work or organized living room concerts like I had planned. I just don't have that sense of urgency behind it, so if today was my last day, then I wouldn't regret not doing it.

For paragliding, the path ahead seemed rather straightforward: do a tandem flight to confirm that I really want to do it, then get a license and buy the equipment. With psychology, I was struggling a bit. There were so many different options with substantial impact on my life path, from going back to university for a degree, to getting certain coaching certifications or combining it with other activities like therapeutic theater. I didn't know what to do with these options; nothing jumped out at me from the page, so I decided to park it for the time being. While I might not have found my way around what to do with my interest in psychology; the whole exercise still gave me a lot of structure in life. My work in the past few years had actually made a difference. Countless written reflections, therapy, listening to my emotions, and asking myself what would be good for myself didn't just improve my awareness of emotions and needs, it also improved my understanding of who I was. I wasn't quite there yet completely (are you ever?), but I was able to imagine a life that at least roughly matched with my strengths and interests. However, I still wasn't ready to find my actual purpose, but more about that later.

The flying ostrich

Fast-forward to a Saturday about 18 months later. I had gotten my paragliding license and found friends to hike and fly with: Markus & Simon. It was May, so we didn't expect there to be any snow left when we chose the mountain to be scaled. But to our surprise, there was snow all the way down to the parking lot, turning knee-deep halfway up. The heavy snow took its toll on our energy levels, to the point that our two hour hike turned into an ordeal four hours long.

Once we reached the top, our focus on safety considerations for a successful takeoff determined the mood. There are always questions that are difficult to answer for comparably inexperienced paragliders. Are we considering all regional and local wind factors when assessing the terrain? Can we get to the landing site from here? Or, the oddest of them all: are we going to make it over that tree line right after the start? In two separate incidents, we actually didn't make it and had to awkwardly turn and land onto the takeoff-site and look for a different slope to get airborne from. Today, however, we didn't encounter any such issues. We quickly settled on a takeoff site, and mostly discussed our hopes for catching thermals as they might be able to lift us higher above the landscape instead of "just" gliding back down within a few minutes.

Generally, we were talking a lot more about thermals than actually catching them though. And it quickly seemed like this time would be no different.

As soon as we flew over the edge after taking off, we found ourselves in a sinking air mass. We didn't have much height to fall through to begin with and the trees below were quickly coming closer. I caught a breeze on takeoff so I still had a few moments to spare before I would have to look for an emergency landing. Markus, however, looked like he was seconds away from hanging in a tree on the side of the mountain. "Teabag" is what we jokingly called paragliders hanging from trees or power lines. You do not want to be a teabag. With winds coming from the east, it was likely that we were already on the lee side of the ridge ahead of us. That would explain the quick sink we found ourselves in. Since we didn't have much height left, we turned straight towards the shortest path to the valley. Markus made it into the steeper terrain without having to land, while Simon started flying in circles in front of me. That must mean that he found a thermal! I followed him and quickly started feeling the lift myself. Flying - and rising - in the same thermal, in the same pillar of air, with a fellow paraglider is one of the greatest experiences of companionship. Within minutes we got up to the cloud base, some 1.5oo meters above the valley floor.

How does one express the beauty of flight artistically? I once went to a concert by an aspiring Irish artist who had asked herself the same question. She had apparently run into trouble finding an appropriate response to the question, as she still asked that same question in the lyrics of the song while moving the backside of her hand up and down the entire keyboard of the piano. I promised myself that if I ever had to ask myself the same question, I would find a better way of expressing it. And now look at me, simply sharing this story. Maybe she didn't do such a bad job after all, considering how memorable of an experience it was.

Anyways. I made it! Me, the big fat burdening ostrich, light as a feather, flying above it all, with hawks as my companions and alpine mountain ridges as my scenery. I think paragliding is a ridiculous sport. All you have is a light seat, a few strings and a piece of plastic cloth above your head, all in all less than 5kg of weight in my case. And just with that you can put five Eiffel Towers worth of height between you and the ground. I started crying. The intensity of the beauty was just overwhelming. Yes, the landscapes are marvelous and I have quite the view up here... but it's more than that. My body was completely irrelevant, unbound by gravity. My history was equally irrelevant. It just didn't matter. I had to pay full attention to the present. Any other worries just faded away. All that was left of me was... just me. Pure experience. Bliss.

The World in Flow

Part III

Chapter Twelve

Who am I not?

The dust and the stones of the street were as precious as gold, the gates were at first the ends of the world. The green trees when I saw them first, through one of the gates, transported and ravished me.... Boys and girls tumbling in the street, and playing, were moving jewels. I knew not that they were born or should die. But all things abided eternally as they were in their proper places. Eternity was manifest in the light of day...

Thomas Traherne[1]

First of all, I ought to explain why the psychological part came first. Life comes with incredible hardships and challenges. When there are financial troubles, a family member is sick or global crises are weighing us down, it is more urgent to find a *modus operandi*

---

1. Quoted in Wilber (1979): No boundary

to deal with life, instead of asking the big questions like "*who am I?*", "*why am I?*" or "*what kind of god would allow this suffering?*". Once we have sufficiently learned to deal with the turmoils of our own lives, we can - if we want to - start uncovering what's beneath. Some people heal sufficiently through their experiences and build stable relationships, do well in their work environments and are generally happy and content with the way things are going. And that's okay. Good for them! But for some people - including me - it goes more like this: I set a goal, I work towards it and do everything to achieve it. Once I do achieve it, there is a short celebratory period of euphoria and subsequent relaxation. And then the existential dread and void kicks in again. *Another* rank at work, *another* mountain climbed, *another* piece learned on the piano. And then what? Is this all there is to it? Is this what life is about? Just swinging like Tarzan from goal to goal, from achievement to achievement, gradually increasing responsibility and the perceived meaning that comes with added responsibility? Do we just have to "*find something worth suffering for*", as Jordan Peterson puts it? If you find yourself asking these questions, the next part of this book is for you!

On the foundation laid out until now, we will hopefully have the capacity to ask the questions that go beyond our psychological, scientific understanding of identity discussed in the first part of the book. So far, almost everything we've read has revolved around the mind, its subconscious and the body. Now we will expand our scope of view to a more global, universal type of consciousness that is more concerned with processes that are not traditionally allocated to the definition of "I".

Traces of experiences of a sort of universal consciousness can be found in all major religions, be it Hinduism, Buddhism, Christianity, Judaism, Islam or Taoism. *The truth is one [and the same] but the sages have given it different names,* as it says in the Rig Veda, a collection of ancient Vedic Sanskrit hymns. The so-called Perennial Philosophy is dedicated to the comparative study of the shared truth among different religions and spiritual paths, collecting significant amounts of evidence of this idea[2]. It also bears resemblance to ideas found in *Advaita Vedanta,* a Hindu path of spiritual practice. With some respect for historic and cultural context, similar descriptions of the universal peace within can be found. Examples of this from different religions include Al-Insān al-Kāmil, Adam Kadmon, the Atman-Brahman or Tathagatagarbha, though there are many more. In the Bible it says: "*It is no longer I who live, but Christ who lives in me*"[3]. Jesus also says: "*I am the light which is on them all. I am the All, and the All has gone out from me and the All has come back to me*"[4]. R.M. Bucke, a psychiatrist in the second half of the 19th century, describes the experience he had after an evening of fruitful discussions and readings of Walt Whitman, among others, as follows:

"*All at once, [...] I found myself wrapped around as it were by a flame-colored cloud. For an instant I thought of fire, some sudden conflagration in the great city; the next, I knew that the light was within myself. [...]. Upon my heart fell one drop of Brahmic Bliss, leaving thenceforward for always an aftertaste of heaven. I saw and knew that the cosmos is not dead matter but a living presence, that the soul of man is immortal, that the universe is so built and ordered that without any peradventure all things work together for the good of each and all, that*

---

2. E.g. Huxley (1945): The Perennial Philosophy

3. Galatians 2:20, English Standard Version

4. Thomas Gospel, 77

the foundation principle of the world is what we call love and that the happiness of every one is in the long run absolutely certain[5] .

From an "outside" perspective, a man in this state appears like this: "*he was now able to enjoy the normal conscious state of man. For he came to see the Mother not only in the ecstatic trance, but all around him in the affairs of man and nature. The frenzy of separation abated and we find a man at ease with the world*"[6] . How does this loving embrace with the entire universe feel exactly? What does it mean? What can we do to get there? And how can it support us with our day-to-day problems beyond the tools in the first part of the book? Does it contain a solution for the aforementioned post-success existential dread?

There are several complications in examining and discussing this universal consciousness with mere words. Words are a part of a relative, temporary existence (which we will elaborate on soon). Words are not able to fully capture the absolute, eternal existence of whatev-er-you-want-to-call-it: God, love, the eternal witness, eternal being, universal consciousness. Buddha puts it this way: "*Don't try to mea-sure with words what is immeasurable [...]. He who asks is wrong, he who answers is wrong*"[7] . We are bound to encounter paradoxes when attempting to illustrate the essence of life with words alone. I could argue that "*there is no you*" and "*everything is you*" and still be fully convinced of both statements at the same time.

Scientific objectivity is based on the assumptions that we are sep-arate entities, and that it is necessary to remove the observer from the

---

5. Bucke (1901): Cosmic consciousness

6. Neveel (1976): The Transformation of Sri Ramakrishna

7. At the Sermon of Benares, quoted in: Institut Saint Christophe (2001): Entre Ciel et Terre [French]

equation. These assumptions have helped us a great deal in advancing society. However, removing the subjective experience robs us of the most important factor in this endeavor. We are essentially buying scientific insight at the cost of ignoring our own role in the equation[8]. Philosophers of ancient Greece had two fitting words for this dichotomy: *mythos* and *logos*. The *logical* refers to things that are empirically comprehensible, while the *mythical* refers to levels of existence that remain hidden to empirical research. They are only accessible through inner observation and experience. To gain a complete understanding, we have to rely on both[9].

Another aspect that complicates our search for understanding in this matter is the historical inaccuracy of religious scripts. Abraham and Moses probably never existed, the Exodus story as well as the tumbling of the walls of Jericho probably never occurred. And King David was probably more of a provincial leader than the king who turned Jerusalem into a mighty capital[10]. That, however, does not mean that we cannot learn from the scripts of the old sages, as at least a good part of the essence of their teachings is still captured in these texts. Peterson for example works with archetypes when studying religious scripts[11]. These are patterns that can be observed in all societies and

---

8. See Jung (1955): Mysterium coniunctionis, p.674

9. For this and the following paragraph see Risi (2004): Licht wirft keinen Schatten [German], p.17, p.357

10. Massing in the New York Times (2002): As Rabbis face facts, bible tales are wilting

11. See Peterson (1999): Maps of Meaning

all mythical stories independent of historic or cultural context[12]. A humble approach with questions like "*What can I learn from this?*" or "*How can this concept be transferred to modern times?*" will help uncover the many treasures waiting to be found in ancient scripts.

Who am I not?

> "*The fundamental experience of human suffering is the experience of alienation from the self, from the source—from God [...] we don't believe the problem is sin, or guilt, or wrongdoing. It's simply misidentification!*"

Amrit Desai, quoted by Stephen Cope[13]

> "*You are not your job. You're not how much money you have in the bank. You're not the car you drive. You're not the contents of your wallet. You're not your fucking khakis. You're the all-singing, all-dancing crap of the world.*"

---

12. See Jung (1959): The Archetypes and the Collective Unconscious

13. Cope (1999): Yoga and the Quest for the True Self, p.62

Tyler Durden in Fight Club[14]

You are not who you think you are. We have become so accustomed to think that we are our thoughts, feelings and bodies that we are completely unaware of our true nature. We learned that an identity is a "*collection of particularities that characterize an entity [..] and distinguish it as an individual from others*". At least according to Wikipedia that is. You like that bright red, brand new Porsche in your driveway, don't you? It *characterizes* you. It *distinguishes* you from your neighbors. You *identify* with it. We commonly identify with all sorts of things - our thoughts, our careers, our countries, our social circles, our bodies. There's just one minor problem with this line of thinking. It is built on the preconception of you as a separate entity. It subtly includes the rough understanding that some collection of stuff commonly understood as "you" makes you some form of entity. Where does the *you* end and the *outside world* begin? Can you pin-point it? When you identify with your car, is it a part of *you?*

Philosophers, spiritual practitioners as well as psychologists have been looking for this exact boundary for centuries, if not millennia. Over time, they have come to different conclusions as to where exactly this boundary supposedly is. Freud stayed around the commonly un-derstood personality and mind with Psychoanalysis, while Jung used mythical archetypes to introduce the idea of a less separated, some-what connected, collective unconscious that is connected to the self, or that constitutes a part of it. As we have seen in this book, modern psychotherapeutic methods also lay great emphasis on the integration of the body into experiences of the "I". You might also already have encountered the principles of *attachment* and *detachment*, originating in Zen Buddhism, that discuss this topic. When you identify with your job or your car, you are *attached* to it, and then when you lose your job or your car breaks down, a part of you *dies*. You suffer. This is what Tyler Durden means when he says: "*The things you own end up owning you*". Your identity has to undergo painful (and unnecessary) changes. You are no longer the person with *that job* or *that car*. Ken Wilber beautifully argues that there are no boundaries at all in his accordingly-named book "No Boundaries"[15]. That there is no separate (id-)entity at all, no "you" compared to an "outside world". But what does this "limitlessness" mean? And how does it fit together with the aforementioned, gross misidentification as the apparent cause of human suffering? If I am so limitless, how could I be alienated from myself?

Who am I not? - An Illustration

6:25pm. Some time between 5pm and 8pm, a thunderstorm was supposed to unload. Right now everything is quiet. At the most, it looks like there's a thin cloud cover with little wind blowing about. There was no sign of any storm on the horizon. Max and me are on the boat, going for a chill cruise. He had the idea of picking up his Tesla that was charging about 15 minutes of paddling down the shoreline. I would then have to paddle the boat back to base by myself. We thought of turning around twice and both times it felt like the right thing to do. I'm aware of the expected storm, and somewhat knowledgeable of meteorological

---

15. Wilber (1979): No Boundary

systems. I know that weather changes can occur extremely fast - especially in the case of thunderstorms.

Except, I liked the thought of having to paddle back by myself in the race against time and nature. It would feel exciting and it would make for a cool story, to bring Max to his electric car by boat. The future of mobility is now! The story was more important than the gut feeling. I was identifying with the story and with being able to tell it. I like storytelling and I like attention. Ultimately, the thrill (and subsequently what other people thought of it) was more important than calm, intuitive decision making. This is action motivated by misidentification.

This action was duly punished accordingly. Shortly after I turned around and began to paddle back, I saw the dark clouds brewing in front of me, quickly moving towards me and the lake. They had been behind us the whole time. Whoops.

Essentially, dark clouds are often full of water, which absorbs more light, making them darker. These clouds are more likely to generate powerful rainfall or storms. Still, there was barely any wind and it would take me maybe another 10 minutes to get back, so I was fairly calm at this point. A water guard then approached me, warning me about the incoming storm and offering to pull me back. It was a bizarre scene. Me, in the little paddle boat which, apart from the guard, was the only boat to be seen far and wide - paddling against both time and the power of mother nature.

To his offer of being pulled, I (still...) just shrugged my shoulders and was like: "uh. I don't think I need it. I mean...if you really want to...". He wanted to. He started circling me, failing to get a hold of my rope. Within seconds, gusts appeared at up to 60km/h. The waves picked up and started dancing. The wind whipped the droplets of lake water across my face as if it wanted to slap me for my silly decision making. The two deck chairs on the back of the boat suddenly flew away without even saying goodbye. I'm in trouble. I'm cowering, dearly holding on to my phone and my shirt, while the wet wind has no mercy in further hitting me in the face. Finally, the water guard is able to pick up the rope at the front of my boat and starts pulling me towards safety. Once we get closer to shore, things calm down a bit. Finally, I made it to shore safely with two deck chairs less and a rather uncomfortable experience gained. Lesson learned, mother nature, lesson learned.

I am not what I observe

In Eastern philosophies, we often come across the phenomenon of temporary appearances as opposed to a stable reality, our "true nature and self". In the Bhagavad Gita, one of the most influential scripts in Hinduism, the main protagonist Arjuna, a warrior plagued by guilt in the face of a battle against his own kin, is taught by Krishna. He learns that his problem is not guilt, but a veil of illusion. That his confused mind can no longer discriminate between this stable reality and temporary appearances. For the temporary, think of feelings, emotions, things, our bodies. Everything that can be perceived. Everything that is bound by space and time. Sri Ramana Maharshi, a Hindu Advaita Vedanta sage, says:

> *"The gross body which is composed of the seven humours,*
> *I am not;*
> *the five sense organs which apprehend their respective*

objects, I am not;
even the mind which thinks, I am not. [16]

The "stable reality" is best captured by the biblical statement of "*I am he who is*", or "*I am who I am*", depending on the translation. This is extremely difficult, if not impossible, to put into proper words as its only characteristic is the fact of existence. Sri Ramana considered this to be the best term for the supreme being, better than those found in Hindu scripts. It is that which cannot be perceived, because it is the perceiver itself. An existence that is beyond space and time, in the eternal now of consciousness.

Okay, but... just because my feelings and all of these other things are temporary, why can I not "be" my feelings, too? Even if they come and go. Maybe my self is just as temporary as all of this? I mean, maybe I will die together with my mind and my body and then that's it? How can we objectively, scientifically verify this whole "*I am not my body, not my feelings, not my mind*" thing? At best, there is anecdotal evidence for things like reincarnation of people who, for example, could remember stories at a young age that were impossible for them to know[17]. There are also interesting aspects to quantum theory arguing for a certain connectedness; we will look at these in later chapters. But in the context of this identity question specifically? I don't think we *can* objectively verify this. I think this is *mythical* knowledge -

---

17. See for example TV shows like "Life, Death and Reincarnation" or "The Ghost Inside My Child" or Tucker (2013): Return to Life: Extraordinary Cases of Children Who Remember Past Lives

something that we have to experience ourselves. Let's now take a look at an exercise for creating this experience.

Exercise I[18]

In the initial chapters of the book around consciousness and emotions, we first came across the idea that our emotions are not "us". Emotions come and go. They *arise in us like clouds and lightning arise in the sky.* Look at feelings that you currently associate with people, places, things, memories or plans. Don't get lost in them, just ponder on them one by one. Look at them with attentive curiosity, without any value judgement. Look at them as you would look at a strange insect walking in the grass. Feel that you are distinct from these emotional currents. There is you, and there are feelings. You are the *perceiver* and your feelings are the *perceived.* You are not your feelings. You just *exist,* while feelings are fleeting, unstable and temporary - like clouds and lightning in the sky. However, just understanding this rationally will get us nowhere; it will just help to boast our ego for having read some fancy concepts in some fancy book, which would be moving in the complete opposite direction: identifying with things that are not our true nature. Deep transformation can only be achieved through steady practice and experience. Feelings are fleeting, unstable and temporary. Can you feel it?

The cool thing is that we can also expand this exercise to everything else commonly associated with identity: our thoughts, our mind, our

---

18. The following exercises are taken from the Maieutique perspectives and adapted

body, our attachments (as part of our feelings). If you focus on the body, what can you observe? What can you feel? Feel the pressure of your seated body on the points where the weight is resting. Feel the texture of the clothes on your skin. Feel the rhythm of breathing and the air penetrating your lungs. Become aware of the air around you, feel it in your face. Pay attention to your blood circulation. Perceive the warmth of its inner movement. Become aware in a general way of this body's life. You are the silent witness of this seated body. Regular practice of observation in this manner will increase the feeling of being the observer and not the observed body itself. A feeling of deep calm and peaceful love will come up and grow, little by little.

You can also contemplate your thoughts - or whatever happens inside you - in a similar fashion. There is you, the observer - and there are thoughts that can be observed. You can even observe the thought "*I observe my thoughts*". Or the thought "*I am observing the thought that I observe my thoughts*", or the thought... okay, you get the point. There are no right or wrong thoughts, no judgement. Only observation of the thoughts as they come and go, nothing else. Observation can be conducted in all sorts of circumstances: When you are working, walking, speaking. Though admittedly, this might be a little advanced. I think especially in the beginning, it is easier to evoke the feeling of being the observer and feel the calmness when you are specifically taking time to sit down and contemplate, rather than when busy at work.

You'll realize that everything in you, desires, fears or regrets, are actually outside of you. Once you stop identifying with your worries, they will not be worries anymore. They will just be clouds that come and go. They are simple perceptions that just move across the field of your view; some of them may be less comfortable than others.

Everything you can observe you are not. You are the observer, not the observed.

Osho shared a wonderful anecdote to illustrate this disregard for worry, when one is not (mis-)identified with matters:[19]

"A great philosopher and world-renowned mathematician is sitting in an airplane. He is sitting in his seat thinking about profound mathematical problems when suddenly the captain makes an announcement, "I am sorry, but we are going to have a slight delay. One of our engines has failed, and we are only flying with three engines."

About ten minutes later, another announcement follows, "I'm afraid we're going to have another delay - two more engines are down, and we only have one left."

Then the philosopher turns to the man sitting next to him and says, "Good Lord! If the next one breaks down too, we'll be sitting up here all night!"

I am non-dual

---

19. Osho (2001): Awareness [Anecdote taken from the German version of the book and translated]

Life is a double-edged sword. Everything that is spatial or temporal seems to appear in pairs. Long vs short, inside vs outside, day vs night, wave vs particle, autonomy vs attachment or future vs past. The same applies to matters that we generally strive for in society. Good vs evil, life vs death, pleasure vs pain, rich vs poor, smart vs dumb etc. In "*The Art of Loving*" Fromm argues that since Aristotle, the Western world has been adhering to the cornerstones of Aristotle's philosophy of logic:

- A is equal to A (day is equal to day)

- A is not equal to non-A (day is not equal to non-day, or night)

- A cannot be A and non-A at the same time(It cannot be day and night at the same time)

A characteristic cannot be attributed to and denied from the same thing at the same time. This does seem to be in line with how the Western world tries to solve problems. Habitually, we have come to think that achieving one side of a pair implies the absence of the opposite of the same pair. If we achieve good, we defeat evil; If there is day, there is no night; if we become rich, we no longer have to deal with the problems of poverty. We take this opposition as a given and then try to manipulate the ends of the spectrum in our favor. Despite the obvious advancements made in fields like medicine and agriculture, we don't appear to be making any progress in this endeavor. Loneliness, anxiety, meaninglessness, wars, pandemics and droughts, among many other problems, are rather present in today's world.

In contrast to this thinking stands the paradoxical logic, introduced by Fromm in "*The Art of Loving*", that is (according to him) dominating in China, India and with Heraclitus, a Greek philosopher: A and non-A can be a part of X at the same point in time. It can be day and night at the same time. I even want to go one step further and say that A and non-A *are* indivisibly both a part of X at the same point in time, not just that they *can be*. Laozi said that *"truly real words are paradoxes"*[20] . In Heraclitus' words, *"one and the same is manifested in things as living and dead, awake and asleep, young and old"* [21] . The pairs of opposites are both inseparably just two sides of the same coin. In Wilber's words, striving for progress implies a discontent with current affairs[22] . In the Tao-Te-Ching it also says: *"When people see things as beautiful, ugliness is created. When people see things as good, evil is created"*. If there was no night, the meaning of a day would be completely lost on us. Clinging to life brings with it a fear of death. Being happy about the arrival of the weekend usually comes with a certain frustration about Monday and the beginning of the new work week. Freedom increases inequality. The freedom to make decisions empowers us to differentiate ourselves from other people making different decisions - and therefore to build wealth. That wealth cannot be considered wealth however, if there are no others

---

20. Laozi: Tao-Te-Ching, Saying 78

21. Heraklit: Fragments, quoted in Fromm (1956): The Art of Loving

22. Wilber (1979): No Boundaries

that are poor in comparison, as a consequence of their own freedom in decision making[23].

> *"Thus, those who say that they would have right without its correlate, wrong; or good government without its correlate, misrule, do not apprehend the great principles of the universe, nor the nature of all creation. One might as well talk of the existence of Heaven without that of Earth, or of the negative principle without the positive, which is clearly impossible. Yet people keep on discussing it without stop; such people must be either fools or knaves"*

Chuang Tzu[24]

We spend our entire lives trying to reach one side of the coin while ignoring the other. We want to "manipulate duality" for these things that we identify with, or that we consider to be important, or a part of ourselves. We are essentially chasing ghosts, negating our true nature - the eternal observer - while the manifested life is temporary and dual. Everything that is dual, you are not. You are the silent witness of duality. Wanting good without accepting bad, wanting happiness while not allowing sadness, is wanting the impossible. You can never

---

23. This line of thinking negates the influence of demographic factors on poverty and is not meant to touch on socioeconomic discussions. The thought is inspired by J. Peterson, e.g. in his podcasts with Joe Rogan.

24. Quoted in Wilber (1979): No Boundaries, p. 22

experience pleasure, except in contrast to pain. If there were no times or states of discomfort then you would never be able to *understand* and *experience* pleasure.

Remember what we said in the beginning of the book, that humans are absolute beasts in the art of adaptation? We just get used to things so quickly. People bound to wheelchairs after accidents are likely to be as happy or discontent with their life as any other person in the population, once a few months have passed since the incident.[25] If you take this insight in the other direction, there is no outside possession or achievement that will make you eternally euphorically happy. If you suddenly drastically had a higher standard of life, or much higher income, or anything else you could wish for, like a partner, social status, a good job etc., you would most likely simply get used to it and return to your "usual" level of content and happiness within months. Naval Ravikant, the author of "How to Get Rich (without getting lucky)", hints at this in his Twitter summary, writing: "*When you're finally wealthy, you'll realize that it wasn't what you were seeking in the first place. But that's for another day*".

So what do we do with this information? Life seems meaningless, we might as well be apathetic and lethargic and not do anything, because in the end, we are just chasing ghosts anyways? From a psychological point of view: No, not at all. Meaninglessness would be the death of drive, cheerfulness and self-worth. If there is no point in doing good (or no way to do so, since it would just be a part of the good vs evil game...), then we would certainly not think that we are "capable of good" or "deserve good". Independent of these philosophical and spiritual considerations, we can still reasonably increase our quality of life, achieve personal growth and healing or provide for a family. We

---

25. Post, Noreau (2005): Quality of Life after Spinal Cord Injury

can still enjoy the perceptions moving across the field of our view, even if we are not identified or caught up in them.

From a spiritual point of view: the question of meaninglessness is even less apparent. There is something that *transcends* this duality: the feeling of deep calm, peace and love that originates from our inner self, once we become more aware of it. This is why it is so incredibly important to experience and not just rationally understand the concepts. The more we become aware of our true nature, the more questions like these simply fade out, because meaning is so deeply felt and perceived. Transcending does *not* mean to negate duality, or deny its existence. A self-realized person is not above or outside of duality, but rather just not *ensnared* and *captivated* by it. The ocean is not above or outside of the waves, but rather just not concerned with how the waves are dancing on the surface. Nonetheless, the ocean and the waves are jointly present at all times - they don't exclude each other.

In eastern scripts, one finds the principle of "desireless action"[26], describing the actions that a person takes when not identified with the material, temporary world, but instead only with the universal consciousness. In this context, Krishna says to Arjuna:

> *Man does not become karmaless (without action)*
> *by simply renouncing actions or by not doing them,*
> *because a man cannot live even for a second*
> *without doing some action.*
> *The mental currents create actions in man at all*
> *times.*

---

26. E.g. Huzur Maharaj Sawan Singh (1963): Philosophy of the Masters, Volume 1

One who forcibly suppresses his physical self
from performing actions is deceiving himself;
for his mind cannot be restrained permanently
in this manner.
Therefore, that person is really great
who conquers his mind by withdrawing it
from worldly desires
and thus acts with disinterest as far as the fruit of action
is concerned,
but interested in serving the Lord only.
He performs his prescribed duties
as indicated in his moral or religious code,
because to act is far better than not to act.
The body
is given to us for the purpose of action,
both internal and external.

Bhagavad Gita[27]

Serving the lord does not mean to serve some imaginary big old beard-ed man sitting above the clouds, but to serve the universal conscious-ness found within everything and everyone. To be a servant to society and the world. To be a servant to your true self. The identification with the old, separated "I" has disappeared and has been replaced by identification with the universal being. Something that would usually be considered "selfless action" is suddenly full of self - full of the universal, eternal self. Regarding the "moral or religious code" that is mentioned here: The Maieutique perspectives tell us that moral

consciousness is a natural companion of growing presence to oneself[28]
. We become creators of our own moral values, providing us with a
spontaneous and adequate response to every situation. We also become more aware of our own negative, semi-unconscious behaviors
and simply stop. This will lead to total spontaneity, from which the
reasoning mind is absent. Life can be extremely simple when there is
no need to make plans, calculate or worry. A first step towards desireless action and the transcendence of duality is achieving outcome
independence. Whenever there is a situation that occupies my mind, I
strive to accept every possible outcome of the situation, while still doing everything in my power for the best possible outcome. When I am
struggling with a (possible) outcome, I can subsequently contemplate
what it is that I'm attached to. We are only free of what we can create
and destroy at the same time[29].

I am not temporal[30]

Quit... don't quit
Noodles... don't noodles
You are too concerned with
what was and with what will be

---

28. Maieutique, Perspective 5

29. Lama Govinda in: Weber (1986): Scientists and Sages

30. See Wilber (1979): No Boundary - Chapter: The No-Boundary
    Moment

Master Oogway[31]

Now it has been mentioned several times that this universal consciousness is "eternal" or "outside of space and time" or "timeless". But what is this supposed to mean exactly? It's not about merely ignoring the past and the future or trying to escape them. They simply don't exist. The only thing that ever *is*, is the eternal now. Think of the past. Can you *perceive* it with your senses? Can you hear it, see it or smell it? You can't, can you? You might be able to remember it. But even your memory is just an experience in the present moment. The future is also just a concept in your head. This is why procrastination is so powerful: tomorrow is *always* one day ahead, no matter how many days you wait. Unless you magically change your attitude overnight. Unless you decide to do things *now* instead of *tomorrow*, you will never get them done. The only time where you can solve problems or do anything else is in the now. And even then you can really only do three things: accept a situation, change what is within your power, or leave the situation. Life is quite simple once the mind's complications are dissolved.

One more thing: *Trying* to contact "the now" or the present moment doesn't make sense. It implies that "the now" is not fully present already. That there is something that has to happen first so that in some imaginary future now you'll be able to access it. However, this future now will never arrive - it is here and has been here the whole time. You don't have to learn or to try or to do anything. There is no way to reach something that already *is*. It is not some specific experience you might have in the future - it is the inherent nature of *every* experience that you have, now and always. This is one of the greatest paradoxes of them all: the necessity of *doing* implies the existence of time and some form of *change* that needs to happen before we can reach the now. While *not doing* ..well.. we would just remain as we are today, wouldn't we?

This perfectly illustrates the shortcoming of words in trying to describe universal, eternal consciousness. This is why Sri Ramana Maharshi says: "*There is neither creation nor destruction; neither destiny nor free-will; neither path nor achievement; this is the final truth*". Any and all of those things would imply that the present moment is not omni-present and timeless and perfect already. We just need to stop resisting and moving away from it. But even that implies the necessity of action again, which is... well... just not true. We are perfect already. Universal consciousness is timeless and inherent to all life already.

This whole concept of time is also the reason for the first part of the book about psychology. You might remember that *being traumatized means [...that] every new event is contaminated by the past.* Let's assume we had a car accident. If we come across a car we don't just see that car. We also see fear, pain or even guilt about what happened. The trauma and the experience resurfaces through triggers like resemblance of the original situation.

Technically speaking, even this "contamination" and the impacts of trauma in the present are also just perceptions moving across the field of our view. Things we can contemplate and use to become aware of the distinction between the observer and the observed. And if we do, we will even detach from these feelings, observe them, solve them, heal them, and suffer less. However, it just makes *perceiving* and "being the observer" somewhat more challenging if everything that we perceive is tainted by a dark past that keeps haunting us. Personally I prefer to also heal my trauma with the tools sourced from psychology and medicine, and then mostly perceiving a car when practicing observation, rather than also perceiving fear, pain and guilt every time I see a car. Either way, the befriending of our inner experiences discussed in the first part goes hand in hand with the practice of observation discussed in the spiritual part of the book.

What is dead may never die

First you have to give up. First you have to know, not fear, know, that someday, you're gonna die. It's only after we've lost everything that we're free to do anything.

Tyler Durden in Fight Club[32]

I let go. Lost in oblivion. Dark and silent and complete. I found freedom. Losing all hope was freedom

Main protagonist in Fight Club

If you spent some time with the exercise in prior chapters, then I hope your alarm bells rang when reading that first quote. You're gonna die? You cannot die. You are eternal, remember? Only the one who thinks he is a human being can believe that he was born, dies

---

32. In the Book/Movie Fight Club (1996 and 1999 respectively)

or is reincarnated, that he goes to paradise or hell[33] . Nonetheless, the body *will* die at some point in time and with it, we will leave behind all the perceptions that we worked so hard to acquire. The sooner we realize that we cannot *keep* or *own* anything forever or take anything with us, the more freedom we gain. Think of the principle of *outcome independence* that was introduced earlier, as a step towards transcending duality and inner peace. Having accepted every possible outcome when going into a situation will make it much more bearable and enjoyable. Now imagine a 100% outcome independence for life in general. Imagine the incredible radiance of calmness and inner peace that this would bring to life. You could go into every situation, into every conversation with a calm, confident smile. This is what accepting death leads to. When you have accepted death, you have accepted pretty much everything that is in between, too. Imagine the shame of walking down the busiest shopping street in your city completely nude. Shame, maybe damage to your reputation or a criminal citation - all things that you cannot take with you after death. So... It's not worse than dying is it? You will be okay. Huzur Maharaj Sawan Singh says: "*Death is not to be feared. It is only the name given to the phenomenon of the soul leaving the body. In Persian this phenomenon is called intiqal, which means transfer. It is merely the withdrawal of the soul from the gross senses, and its entrance into finer regions. It is merely giving up the present garment, namely, the body. It does not mean annihilation. There is life after death, although we may not be able to see it. All saints accept this principle. [...] A person who dies while living*

---

33. Maieutique, Perspective 12

lives forever. One who looks upon life in this world and death with the same attitude, is also free from death"[34].

In meditation, I sometimes ask myself what feelings would arise if I died today. What or whom would I be sad about leaving behind? What are the things I didn't do or didn't say? Is there a passion that I am not following? Am I stuck in the wrong job? How important is it what people think of me? This way I can quite quickly identify attachments, or *misidentification*, or other worldly desires. I can then decide if I want to act on them or just observe them, until I understand them better and they go away. Imagine dying before you told your parents you loved them (I love you mom), or while being stuck in a job that you don't like. Or before doing *that thing* on your bucket list. And just like with everything else that is dual, life and death are two inseparable sides of the same coin. Yielding to death unconditionally, or even just contemplating it, fills life with meaning. Befriending the temporality of things somehow makes us feel so much more alive.

Part of what Sawan Singh writes is that *a person who dies while living lives forever*. What does this mean? Sawan Singh uses a quote from Kabir, an Indian mystic, to elaborate:

> *The whole world keeps on dying again and again,*
> *But no one dies the real death*
> *I have died a death that will make me never die again*

If you have watched it, you might also come to think of the slogan of the Greyjoy family from Game of Thrones:

WHAT IS DEAD MAY
NEVER DIE

Accepting death and with it, the impermanence of life, fuels the process of switching from misidentification with the temporary over to identification with our true, eternal nature. The more we practice, the more we start naturally identifying with the observing consciousness and less with the observed - body, feelings and thoughts. This true self is eternal and will never die. The actual physical death will then just be a perception, moving across the field of your view - and therefore not even be of importance. This is why *what is dead may never die*. When you have accepted the death of your body, you are ready to explore the death-lessness of your true nature. Or, in Tyler Durden's words: *"Maybe self-improvement isn't the answer, maybe self-destruction is the answer"*.

Imagine I died tonight in my sleep. Just didn't wake up tomorrow and that was it. That would be rather inconvenient. Maybe I should tidy my room before that? My friend would have to go to the library tomorrow without me. Maybe he would think that I'm just a no-show. Technically I would be a no-show. Awkward. Maybe dying is a valid excuse? Oh and I still wanted to improve my risotto making skills. Not having to feed myself every couple of hours would be rather convenient, however. It still doesn't seem to come to me naturally.

Anyways. Would I miss the people around me? Yes. No. I don't know. How do emotions work after you die? I think I would be sad about leaving behind all the people that I love. What are they going to do without my silly jokes? Maybe my jokes aren't as important as I think. Mhh... Who would come to my funeral? Who would be invited to it? Who would even organize a funeral? Would people manage to have fun or pull a few dark jokes about me? Would anyone have the guts to roast me in my eulogy? I would like that. I would like to be set ablaze by arrows shot onto a boat on the Danube, like in a viking ritual. Going out in style.

Anything else? I want to achieve an even higher level of radical honesty. To always let people know what I think. To align my actions with my emotions. To align my words with my thoughts. Is there anything that I must still experience in life? Taking a date on a tandem-paraglide would absolutely be a bucket list experience. Maybe learning to do "loopings" in my paraglider? Or playing Liszt's piano version of the "Danse Macabre"? Ensuring that my family never ever has to worry about money again? I'm actively working towards most of the things on this list so... I guess it's fine. Most likely I'm just going to wake up tomorrow anyways.

Chapter Thirteen

Who am I?

Oh, I could sing such grandeurs and glories about you!
You have not known what you are, you have slumbered
upon yourself all your life,
Your eyelids have been the same as closed most of the
time...

Whoever you are! claim your own at any hazard!
These shows of the East and West are tame compared to
you,
These immense meadows, the interminable rivers, you
are immense and interminable as they.

Walt Whitman
"To you"[1]

---

1. Quoted in Cope (1999): Yoga and the Quest for the True Self,

So far we have been looking at our true nature by discussing that which we are not. This is like trying to define light as the absence of shadow. Light is so much more than that. Without light, there would be no shadow. The same goes for us - we are much more than just the absence of the temporary or the dual. So all we have achieved so far is really just an approximation, at best. Now we want to shine more light on who we actually are. On what we have so far called the eternal witness, eternal being, universal consciousness, god, love, that which cannot be perceived, existence beyond space and time, or the *I am*. More religious terms would be Brahman, Tao, Christ, or Nirvana.

Let's now look at the sages' attempts to describe this - *to measure with words what is immeasurable*, as Buddha said it. This way we can slightly refine and sharpen our rough idea of the universal, eternal consciousness before we aim to experience it ourselves with an exercise. Buddha himself described it as *"the non-composed, difficult to see, unshakable, non-curved, immoral, pure, refuge, island, fort, support, protection, the one who does not transmigrate, the non-inflamed, non-burnt, omnipresent, very pure, subtle, peaceful, the one without affliction, the one who has not come to existence"*[2]. Sri Ramana Maharshi's writes about the true self that:*"I am the one who is immanent in all"* and *"Everything that is seen or heard in the universe, inside as well as outside, is penetrated by me"*[3]. In the Tao-Te-Ching it says: *"The Tao is as a gulf out of which all things come"* - *"The Tao itself does not act, however everything is done by him"* - *"The Tao is the secret and common foundation of all beings"* - *"Who is celestial will be one with*

---

2. Budda in the Samyukta Agama Sutra 890. Unfortunately, the only version available online is in traditional chinese:

3. Sri Ramana Maharshi: Atma Sakshatkara 4, 11

the Tao". In Christian texts, we also find the aspects of timelessness ("*Jesus Christ is the same yesterday, today, and forever"*[4]), immanence ("*God's kingdom is inside you"*[5] - "*I live, but it is not me anymore, it is Christ who lives in me"*[6]) and the aspect of love or strong benevolence ("*God is love, and the one who abides in love abides in God, and God abides in him"*[7]). Ibn 'Arabi, a Muslim mystic wrote: "*Without Him as active principle and without us as receptacles of His act, nothing would exist. Indeed I adore Him and God is our Master. But, I am Himself. Be at the same time God in your essence and creature in your form, and you will be by God the dispenser of His mercy"*[8]. In Islam, one of the most fundamental concepts is *Tawhid* (identifying with that which is one).[9] Anything that distracts you from *Tawhid* is considered a sin. This includes egoism as well as striving for money or a higher social status. That sounds similar to what we discussed in prior chapters, doesn't it? The loving nature of consciousness noted before is also addressed in the Maieutique perspectives and by Sawan Singh:

"*When there is attention, lucidity, and mental silence, love springs up. It is a pure source which expresses itself for the pleasure of loving, expecting nothing in return. [..] The more you remain innerly melted in*

---

4. Hebrews 13:8

5. Luke 17-21

6. Paul Galates 4-7

7. John 4-16

8. Ibn 'Arabi: Fusus al-Hikam (the Seal of Wisdom)

9. Rojek (2012): Fame Attack: The Inflation of Celebrity and Its Consequences p. 114

the Transcendental Being, the more love fills you. It is an uninterrupted flow of love which pours over you and towards creation.

Love is not dependent on anything else. It is an ocean of faith and fortitude. It is an ocean of strength and faith. It imparts peace and serenity to the mind and to life. It is of real and lasting value. All the things of this world appear beautiful when there is love. By the currents of love the entire atmosphere is charged with joy, and the spark of God's light is visible in love".

For me, the greatest part of spiritual practice is just observation. Everything else - love, compassion, calmness - comes as a result. Remember when, at the beginning of the book, I said that Buddha's teachings can be summarized with *"love yourself and observe"* and you were probably wondering why I thought that observing is more important than love? This is why. By observing, you can become aware of the observer. The observer is love in its purest form, outside of space and time, outside of the fleeting instability of clouds and lightning in the sky. I don't think we can evoke true, stable, calm love while disconnected from the universal source of it.

Do you remember Branden's definition of confidence? Being capable of good, and deserving good. Successfully identifying with the inner observer actually leads to confidence in this regard. Why? Because you *are* love. How can love not be deserving of love at the core of its being? How could you not be deserving of your own true being - it is what you *are*. And how could love not be capable of good? Isn't love the most powerful thing there is, able to transcend everything else? At your core being, you are eternal. And you transcend everything. Jesus said: *"I am in everything"* and well - that's you. Isn't that powerful? And isn't that deserving of good? You just have to realize that it is the case.

Exercise II

Now, the way you conduct the following exercise of observation is up to you: you can include it as a small part of regular/daily meditation where you ponder these things, or you can spend a lot of time at once on it. You could camp in the wilderness for a few days, without your phone, without other people, without any outside distractions. And then experience what remains of you when you strip away your daily life and surroundings. Or you could do something like a Vipassana retreat, where pretty much everything is forbidden: reading, writing, speaking, interacting, phones, computers, fasting etc. Basically, almost everything except existing is prohibited. This helps you learn to stop resisting the blissful experience of your own existence. You can also use part I of the exercise in the section *I am not what I observe* to warm up and to start calming your mind down, away from the restless noise of daily life.

Who are you? There is no point in answering this question with a ready-made intellectual theory. Repeatedly ask yourself that question and listen to the inner response in the following exercise. Only then can you experience the pure "I". There is nothing the mind can say about it. Because it is devoid of any content. We cannot think about it, but we can perceive it.

Close your eyes. Strip everything away. Forget your body. Forget the world. Forget even the memory of the world. Imagine now that you stop thinking. What remains of you? Verify that you still exist. Perceive your pure existence. Intensify your feeling of existing. Bring your attention to this existence itself. This fact of existing is free from all perceptions and all thoughts. In every instant this fact of existing immutably abides in you. There is silence, void, immobile space. You enter this void and this silence without beginning or end. You enter the knowledge of what is nameless. You realize that the witness has neither form nor limit. This witness is yourself and you experience it.

When you are in a state of deep, dreamless sleep, what remains of you? Only the fact of existing. There is no physical perception, no mental perception or mental consciousness, there is only the Consciousness of the Being without any content. Recall the last time you were in deep sleep. What were you then? Try to feel it. To feel in you the pure Being is to feel something that in this very instant you have in common with deep sleep. Understand that the fact of Existing underlies the states of wakefulness, sleep with dreams and sleep without dreams : these are just different shows.

Now, after having remained in this state with your eyes closed for a while, think of the world again. Raise up in you the desire, the curiosity of seeing its strange appearance again, and slowly open your eyes. Then look at what is in front of you. You are dazzled by thousands of forms and colors. You have come from the total absence of everything and the beauty of the world strikes you. It is the wonderful meeting of the opposites: full and empty, colorful and colorless, limited and unlimited, temporal and intemporal. Life and its phenomenal phantasmagoria become a perpetual delight and ecstasy.

You love the world as man loves woman.

Who knows that, has unending joy.

I was expecting the weather to turn sour, so I left my paraglider at the hut. Hike back down like a mere mortal for once, I thought. However, the weather reports these days were as untrustworthy as a dealer at Praterstern. As we reached the top of the nearby hill, the sun kept shining and there were barely any clouds in sight. The east wind made for perfect starting conditions. On the lee side of the peak, my brother, his girlfriend and I found a quiet place to sit and enjoy the view. Not being occupied with planning a flight, I made use of the opportunity to meditate. My spread out jacket protected me from the tickling grass that likes to dance in the wind. I start by finding a comfortable position and closing my eyes. I feel alive. The ice cold shower I had earlier erased any doubts I might have had about being alive. I can feel my heart pumping, slowly calming down and adapting its tempo to the break. Thoughts are rushing through my head. It was silly not to carry my glider either way. The price of not flying, even though the conditions allow it, was a higher price to pay than having to carry it back down in the event of rain. It's okay, mistakes happen. I don't want to get lost in single streams of thoughts. What else is going on? The events of the last few days are passing before my inner eye. The people I met at the hut, the hiking routes, the flights of the past few days. I shift my attention to become aware of observing. To become aware of the observer of all this day-to-day turmoil. I imagine my body doesn't exist. That I have neither thought nor emotion. I forget the world. I forget even the memory of the world. I verify that I continue to exist. I am. Neither form nor limit. Inherent to all existence. I can fly like a bird above the valley and be wild as a lion in the jungle. The beauty of simply being overcomes me. A calm love for existence springs up. I remain in this state for a bit, while random thoughts come and go, with little glimpses of no thoughts in between.

I raise in myself the desire to see the world again. I imagine the dazzling beauty of a thousand sounds, forms and colors. The interplay of emptiness and fullness. A dream built on a void. The eternal's game. I open my eyes. Insects are buzzing around me. I can hear a plane in the distance. Across the valley the north wall of the Weisseck proudly stands a thousand meters tall. Cumulus clouds are gathering around its peak. Down below, a hiker makes their way on the meandering path. A soft breeze of wind dances around my face. It feels like a dream. A rather enjoyable one, that is. To what can one become attached, if one sees the world as a dream built on a void?

Chapter Fourteen

Suffering &
Spirituality

Psychological mastery as a prerequisite for spiritual progress

Wait, but didn't we spend half of the psychology part of the book on building a strong sense of identity? With *associating* with our characteristics, especially in the accordingly-named chapter? Why are we all of a sudden supposed to undo all of that careful work again and *dissociate*? We thought carefully about what we like and dislike and what our values are, only to learn now that we are just existing and that we should stop identifying with everything that we perceive... that's a bit of back and forth, isn't it? Yep. It is. Let me explain.

You might have noticed that we gradually increased the scope of I. The first part of this book revolves around understanding the organism - the personality, the subconscious, the body. Now we are discussing unity consciousness - our identity in a much broader sense. Doesn't it make sense to master - or at least understand - a smaller scope before moving on to a broader, more advanced scope?

If we jumped straight to the spiritual version of "who am I?", before exploring our likes, values and such, we would probably only learn to *dis*sociate. We would learn to remove ourselves from attachment to the world of temporality, but there is a good chance it would just lead to apathy, lethargy and a deep lack of meaning. This is what happened to me when I first came across these spiritual insights. I *dissociated* in a twisted search for detachment. I didn't *associate* with anything instead. Everything just became grey. If we don't have a strong, solid sense of identity then we have nothing to fall back on while we get to know our true selves, and while we practice the art of observation. Progress is always a tussle of back and forth. One step back, two steps forward. There will be times where all of this seems far-fetched or doesn't make sense or where you just don't *feel* it. In these times it's important to have a life and structure to fall back on. Mastering the psychological part might not grant eternal content and an endless pool of calm love, but it will certainly grant the stability to be generally content through the ups and downs of life.

In the perspectives, it says to "*Stop identifying to man and identify to the infinity. Repeat mentally "this I am" while identifying with the incommensurate*"[1] . If we have never learned to build our identity - to consciously identify with our surroundings, our friends, our values - then how are we going to be able to achieve this? How can we then identify with something that cannot even be described, hardly even

---

1. Maieutique, Perspective 12

perceived? This is difficult enough as is, even with plenty of prior practice in identity-building.

Another crucial skill that is practiced throughout the first part of the book is the art of observation. Consciousness is not the start to the book without reason. If we don't learn to observe, we cannot become aware of (suppressed) feelings and resolve them. We also can't become aware of the observer itself. This is another reason why my first adventure down the rabbit hole ten years prior wasn't very successful. I was trying to observe the observer, while not realizing that there was a mountain of feelings and misguided bonding behavior causing havoc in my life. Unknowingly, I had plenty of habits established whose sole purpose was to *distract* me from observing and becoming aware. I had to learn that my recurring feeling of being unwelcome and abandoned is unresolved trauma that I can heal; I had to build a solid identity that I liked. Only then could I start walking the rewarding path of spirituality.

The silver linings of trauma survivors in the search for our true self[2]

The GULAG Archipelago is a three-volume text about Soviet labour camps written by Aleksandr Solzhenitsyn. Jordan Peterson described it as the most important book of the twentieth century[3]; TIME called it the best non-fiction book of the twentieth century.

---

2. See Risi (2004): Licht wirft keinen Schatten [German], p. 241 ff.

3. Peterson online at

To paint a realistic picture of the horrors of Soviet labour camps, Solzhenitsyn uses a wide range of sources like interviews, diaries and legal documents, as well as his own experience as a GULAG prisoner. He himself endured and survived 11 years of gruesome camp imprisonment. Arrests could happen at random, without any reason or trial. The arrest itself was a sufficient admission of guilt. After all, if you were innocent, why would you have even been arrested in the first place? The interrogations were just as harsh: "*To crush him once and for all and to cut him off from all others once and for all - that was the function of interrogation under Article 58*"[4]. Prisoners would suffer from sleep deprivation, beating to the head, teeth and genitalia, shouting and having thrown stuff against the head. Rape was also a fairly common occurrence: "*Obvious old age and obvious ugliness were the only defenses for a woman there - nothing else. Attractiveness was a curse*"[5]. People around Solzhenitsyn would regularly die of starvation, exhaustion or revolts. You would expect a man having to survive in this environment for several years to be broken, traumatized and yearning for freedom. Yet, as Solzhenitsyn catches a glimpse of freedom and normal life as he changes camps after four years of imprisonment, riding a train with only two guards, he is shocked by his experience:

"*...and you hear strange and insignificant conversations: about some husband who beats up his wife or has left her; and some mother-in-law who, for some reason, does not get along with her daughter-in-law; how neighbors in communal apartments make personal use of the electric outlets in the corridor [...] You listen to all this, and the goose pimples of rejection run up and down your spine: to you the true measure of*

---

4. Solzhenitsyn (1974): The Gulag Archipelago, Volume I, p. 504

5. Solzhenitsyn (1974): The Gulag Archipelago, Volume II, p. 233

things in the Universe is so clear! The measure of all weaknesses and all passions! And these sinners aren't fated to perceive it. The only one there who is alive, truly alive, is incorporeal you, and all these others are simply mistaken in thinking themselves alive. And an unbridgeable chasm divides you! You cannot cry out to them, nor weep over them, nor shake them by the shoulder: after all, you are a disembodied spirit, you are a ghost, and they are material bodies. And how can you bring it home to them? By an inspiration? By a vision? A dream? Brothers! People! Why has life been given you?"[6]

He exhibits the virtues of a man that is deeply rooted and at peace with himself, independent of any imprisonments. About the - usually to be feared - return to prison, he writes:

"And after spending a few hours among free people, here is what I feel: My lips are mute; there is no place for me among them; my hands are tied here. I want free speech! I want to go back to my native land! I want to go home to the Archipelago! [...]

I smile at the first courtyard and recognize the familiar main doors of carved wood. And it's nothing at all to me that they are now going to make me face the wall - and they already have - and ask me: 'Last name? Given name and patronymic? Year of birth?' - My name? I am the Interstellar Wanderer! They have tightly bound my body, but my soul is beyond their power"[7].

He even develops a distinct gratitude about having been to prison:

"All the writers who wrote about prison but who did not themselves serve time there considered it their duty to express sympathy for prisoners and to curse prison. I... have served enough time there. I nourished my

---

6. Solzhenitsyn (1974): The Gulag Archipelago, Volume I, p. 590

7. Solzhenitsyn (1974): The Gulag Archipelago, Volume I, p. 595

soul there, and I say without hesitation: "Bless you, prison, for having been in my life!"

(And from beyond the grave come replies: It is very well for you to say that-when you came out of it alive!)[8]

So how did that happen? What about this environment caused Solzhenitsyn to "*nourish his soul*", as he puts it? What is the connection between difficult experiences and spiritual progress?

Pete Walker captures this spiritual progress as "*emotional intelligence far beyond the norm*"[9]. His explanation is that "*many of us were forced to consciously address our suffering, because our wounding was so much more severe*". Ken Wilber saw the same connection between personal growth and difficult experiences. He writes that "*suffering smashes to pieces the complacency of our normal fictions about reality, and forces us to become alive in a special sense*". If you live a reasonably emotionally and physically healthy and stable life in a developed country, you might come to the conclusion that "everything is fine", and that "these ups and downs are just a normal part of life". This is why the spiritual part of the book might not be for everyone - learning to deal with these ups and downs on an emotional level will just be sufficient.

While, if we have experienced strong forms of suffering, this "complacency of our normal fictions about reality" is smashed to pieces. The identification with objects that are not in line with our true nature is painfully punished by our experiences. We have to - as Wilber puts it - learn to "*see carefully, feel deeply, touch ourselves and the world in ways we have heretofore avoided*". Seeing carefully and feeling deeply

---

8. Solzhenitsyn (1974): The Gulag Archipelago, Volume II, p. 617

9. Walker (2013): Complex PTSD, p. 68

hones the skill of observation. When you spend a lot of time observing, you will sooner or later become aware of the observer - or unity consciousness as Wilber calls it. Love, calmness and maturity will just be natural consequences of this awareness. In the exercises in the spiritual part of this book, we really aren't doing much more than observing various things. *Love yourself and observe*, remember? Wilber writes in this regard that: "*The emergence of suffering is not so much good as it is a good sign, an indication that one is starting to realize that life lived outside unity consciousness is ultimately painful, distressing, and sorrowful*".

A phenomenon that subtly accompanies this whole discussion is dissociation. Dissociation in the spiritual context is basically the separation from the false ego, that has been visited mainly in the sections "*Who am I not*" and "*What is dead may never die*". It generally refers to the conscious dissociation of feelings, thoughts, body, riches, reputation and such, to switch over to associating with the inner, eternal I. Think of the idea "*I am not this body, I am just the observer*" or, similarly "*This is not my body, I am just allowed to fill it with my soul for this lifespan*".

In the context of psychology, dissociation is a coping mechanism in strongly traumatizing situations or environments. It enables the victims to at least flee with their mind, even though they might not be able to escape physically. For example, it can lead victims of abuse to dissociate from the specific memories of their traumatic incidents, meaning they cannot remember what happened. As another example, it can keep people from being able to feel their own body in situations of conflict. Or just a general "zoning out" in uncomfortable situations can also be a form of dissociation as a protective pattern. There are countless more examples of trauma leading to dissociation in various forms; another one around feeling out of touch with reality can be read in the situation described in the section "immediate safety".

Dissociation as an apparent parallel between traumatic incidents and spiritual progress is also captured by Solzhenitsyn. The following paragraph reverberates the spiritual death from the section "*what is dead may never die*", though in this context it is obviously trauma-induced: "*From the moment you go to prison you must put your cozy past firmly behind you. At the very threshold, you must say to yourself: "My life is over, a little early to be sure, but there's nothing to be done about it. [...] I no longer have any property whatsoever. For me those I love have died, and for them I have died. From today on, my body is useless and alien to me. Only my spirit and my conscience remain precious and important to me*"[10] . The positive side effects of the (forced) dissociation and liberation from the fleeting, false "I" also appear in the letter of a fellow prisoner to his fiancée: "*Here all the trivia and fuss have decreased... I have experienced a turning point... here you harken to that voice deep inside you, which amid the surfeit and vanity used to be stifled by the roar from outside*"[11] .

Turning water into wine and suffering into growth[12]

---

10. Solzhenitsyn (1974): The Gulag Archipelago, Volume I, p. 130

11. Solzhenitsyn (1974): The Gulag Archipelago, Volume II, p. 605

12. See Risi (2004): Licht wirft keinen Schatten [German], p. 228 ff.

So does that mean that suffering is good? And people that (want to) cause harm actually do good? It would be the case if you were to believe Mephistopheles in Goethe's Faust:

> *"Ein Theil von jener Kraft,*
> *Die stets das Böse will und stets das Gute schafft."*

> *"Part of the Power that would*
> *Always wish Evil, and always work the Good."*

We have to differentiate here very carefully. To cause harm is the decision and responsibility of the aggressor. He who wants to cause harm, causes harm. The person suffering the attack then has a choice between responding to the aggression or using the harm done for growth, peace and wisdom. The positive impact of doing the latter is only attributable to the person suffering the aggression, but never to the aggressor!

However, giving in to provocation, aggression or (negative) seduction increases the guilt and responsibility of the aggressor, as it increases the actual harm resulting from his actions. And by giving in, I am referring to emotions as much as to actions. Letting a thirst for revenge and hate consume you will be just as bad as acting it out. Not giving in means to not judge but merely differentiate. You can still decide what type of influence you want to have in your life even without judging the other. As the rapper Tupac Shakur said: "*I still wanna see you eat, just not at my table*".

Think of the story of a Jewish lawyer who had his wife and five kids shot by the Nazis right in front of him[13]. He had begged to die with them but was spared because he could speak German. Instead of letting the hate that had killed his family consume him, he decided right then to love every person he ever met. He went on to spend six years in a KZ without showing any signs of sickness or starvation upon his liberation. Even more amazing, he appeared to be friends with every group and nationality of inmates, with inmates' quarrels being brought before him for arbitration. He felt love for his tormentors. How filled with hate they must be and in what a place of darkness they must be!

Ideally, we can find purpose, a lesson and potential for wisdom in all suffering. It can help us to forgive all aggression (without endorsing or approving it, of course). This empathy is a key step towards transcending the duality of good and bad, of action and reaction, of aggression and response that seems to rule this realm. Isn't this also *the* main message of Jesus on the cross? To bear the action without reaction, without hate and without revenge. To wash away the sins of crucifying him because he remains forgiving and loving regardless of what is being done to him.

---

13. The story is difficult to verify. It was told in: Ritchie (1978): Return from Tomorrow, p. 114ff.

Chapter Fifteen

Who are we?

Finding the dots with modern physics (and physicists)

A human being is part of the whole called by us universe, a part limited in time and space. He experiences himself, his thoughts and feelings as something separated from the rest, a kind of optical delusion of his consciousness. This delusion is a kind of prison for us, restricting us to our personal desires and to affection for a few persons nearest to us. Our task must be to free ourselves from this prison by widening our circle of compassion to embrace all living creatures and the whole of nature in its beauty.

Albert Einstein[1]

I celebrate myself, and sing myself,
And what I assume you shall assume,
For every atom belonging to me as good belongs to you.

Walt Whitman

The Tao is a gulf out of which *all* things come. Buddha used the word *"omnipresent"*. Heraclitus said that *"one and the same is mani-fested in things as living and dead, awake and asleep, young and old"*. This unity of consciousness, this connectedness between all things, has subtly surfaced throughout the spiritual part of this book. We asked the question *"where does the you end and the outside world begin?"* and we mentioned the "limitlessness" of no boundaries, that Ken Wilber discusses[2]. Yet, despite this, we mostly talked about "I" as a separate entity. We did this for mere simplicity - to better discuss the aspects of non-temporality, non-duality and of not being what we observe. In this chapter, we want to discuss the aspect of connected-ness more in-depth.

Think of the wave-ocean metaphor that we have come across be-fore. The depth and calmness of the universal ocean, *"out of which all things act"* but that *"itself does not act"*. The waves dancing on the surface which - if you look at them as separate entities - come and go, like all the temporal phenomena of life. It's one of those paradoxes

---

2. Wilber (1979): No Boundaries

in our search for truth. If we look at a single wave, we can clearly define its boundaries. It has a crest and a trough. It will surface and then disappear or crash on the beach. It has a beginning and an end. Accordingly, if we focus on our bodies, our individuality, and our thoughts, we will become convinced of our separation. But if we shift attention to the ocean itself, if we look inside ourselves (and at this chapter) we might be able to see and hopefully feel and understand the connection of all existence.

Matter is like a small ripple on this tremendous ocean of energy, having some relative stability and being man-ifest

David Bohm[3]

Words that have helped me come to terms with the wave-ocean metaphor are "absolute" and "relative". The temporal comings and goings of life are not any less real, despite their ephemerality. They are a way of eternity constantly unfolding itself, just in a *relative* order. Like a game on the computer. It exists, but it's just a relative side of reality. Once you stop playing the game, you are bound to face life again. It's the same with this life - once you stop playing around, once you stop being so concerned with the daily noise of your hamster wheel, you are bound to face the ocean and become aware of your ocean-ness. You are always the ocean and you are always connected; it's just a matter of shifting your attention towards it and becoming aware of it. The ocean is the absolute.

---

3. Weber (1974): Scientists and Sages, p. 52

This interplay between connectedness and a subsequent rooted, playful and joyous individuality comes out in a conversation between Renee Weber and the renowned physicist David Bohm[4]:

Bohm: *Ego-centeredness centers on the self-image, which is an illusion and a delusion. Therefore it's nothing. In true individuality a true being unfolds from the whole in its particular way for that particular moment.*

Weber: *Oddly, one's sense of being rooted in this whole is what permits true individuality.*

Bohm: *Yes. It is impossible to have true individuality except when grounded in the whole. Anything else is egocentrism.*

Weber: *Most people think these are synonymous.*

Bohm: *Anybody who is self-centered must be divided, because in order to become self-centered he must establish a division between himself and the whole.*

Bohm's statements are certainly inspired by the insights in quantum physics that were gained in the first half of the 20th century, when physicists like Schrödinger or Heisenberg realized that the laws of classical physics weren't applicable on the microscopic level of atoms. For example, Heisenberg's uncertainty principle states that you cannot know both the location and the speed of a particle like a photon or electron. The more you determine its location, the less you know about its velocity and vice versa[5]. Heisenberg himself said that: "*...the building-stones of matter [...] defy all forms of objective location in space*

---

4. Weber (1974): Scientists and Sages, p. 30

5. Max Born for example considered the idea that particles were merely probabilities of existence and occurrence, see for example Born (1949): "Natural Philosophy of Cause and Chance"

and time". The idea of fundamentally separated objects was eradicated and replaced by an interwoven, connected web of different unfoldings of energy. As a consequence, *"...the common division of the world into subject and object, inner world and outer world, body and soul, is no longer adequate and leads us into difficulties"*[6] .

This lack of division into subject and object also becomes apparent in the thought experiment of Schrödinger's cat. Only by checking the box, the status of the cat (dead or alive) is determined. It served as a perfect example illustrating that the scientific observer had been replaced by a participator. It's impossible to observe a system without interacting with it. Today's developments in information security make use of this phenomenon. For example, quantum security keys make it impossible to observe communication without interfering with it and therefore render the message useless - thus letting the communicators know that they are being observed.

These ideas reflect the compatibility of modern physics with the spiritual views and ideas held by mystics of all ages and traditions (and expressed at the beginning of this chapter). I don't believe in the principal opposition of mystical insights against logical sciences. Instead, I think they are approximating the same set of insights from different angles. Mystic writings were tempered with, obscured and lost throughout the ages of history, while modern sciences are still only scratching on the surface of how things work. Both narratives are oftentimes exploited for the agendas and goals of individuals. Yet, when distilled, both sides seem to be pointing towards the same set of fundamental ideas.

---

6. Heisenberg (1958): The Physicist's Conception of Nature, p.24

The physicist Fritjof Capra discusses the compatibility of modern physics with spiritual ideas in-depth in his book "The Tao of Physics"[7] :

"The basic oneness of the universe is not only the central characteristic of the mystical experience, but is also one of the most important revelations of modern physics. It becomes apparent at the atomic level and manifests itself more and more as one penetrates deeper into matter, down into the realm of subatomic particles. [...] The constituents of matter and the basic phenomena involving them are all interconnected, interrelated and interdependent; that they cannot be understood as isolated entities, but only as integrated parts of the whole".

"...integrated parts of the whole", "eradicated the idea of fundamentally separated objects" or *"lack of division into subject and object":* We have now discussed the idea of connectedness from a scientific perspective. But unfortunately, as always, just logically understanding concepts is only going to get us so far. Only the mystic experience of it will help us to truly feel them and benefit from them. Let's have a look at how this experience of connectedness might play out in our exercises of observation and day-to-day experiences.

Connecting the dots

In the exercise part I in the section "I am not what I observe", we observed our environment, our feelings, and our body. And we learned that what can be perceived is not the perceiver. *"Everything*

---

7. Capra (1975): The Tao of Physics, p.131

in you, that desires, fears or regrets, is actually outside you"; "You are not your job. You're not how much money you have in the bank..."). We learned that everything that you can observe is outside of you, no matter what it might be. It's difficult to find a difference between seeing your own body or a tree, or a bird. At the end of the day, all of them are just perceptions moving across your field of view. Taking the physical insights into account, everything that I observe might be connected in this *"web of different unfoldings of energy".* But if I'm not any of those things, where does that leave me?

In part II of the exercise in "Who am I?" we tried to shift the focus to who we actually are. We came across the aspects of love (*"When there is mental silence, love springs up..."*) and immanence (*"the gulf out of which all things act", "everything that is seen or heard in the universe, inside as well as outside, is penetrated by me"*). It did however turn out to be rather difficult to go beyond mere observation of our being (the *I am*): *"The one who has not come to existence", "neither form nor limit", "devoid of any content. We cannot think about it, but we can perceive it".*

Let's now apply these thoughts to the process of observing something. On one side you have everything observed. The waves. Feelings, thoughts, body, and objects in your environment. The constant unfolding of energy in a temporary way. On the other side you have the observer. The ocean. Neither form nor limit. Devoid of any content. The gulf out of which all things act. The one who is immanent in all. On one side the observed, on the other the observer. On one side waves, on the other side the ocean. That seems rather dual to me. But what have we learned about duality?

As a quick reminder:

We spend our entire lives trying to reach one side of the coin while ignoring the other. We want to "manipulate duality" for the things we

consider to be important. We are essentially chasing ghosts, negating our
true nature [...]. You are the silent witness of duality.

There is never one without the other. Even being the observer and
being the observed are simply two sides of the same coin. There is only
one thing - the process of observation. The process of existing. The
"process" of love. This is what the following Buddha summary refers
to:

> *Suffering alone exists, none who suffer;*
> *The deed there is, but no doer thereof;*
> *Nirvana is, but no one seeking it;*
> *The Path there is, but none who travel it.*

The path - the process of development and spiritual progress - there
is, in this constant unfolding of waves, but there is no separate you
traveling it. There is only the all-encompassing Tao. Whether you call
it "I", Tao, Brahman, Christ, Energy, or God really doesn't make much
of a difference at this point. This marriage of ocean and waves, of
observer and observed, also becomes apparent in Chuang Tzu's quote:
Actualized men *"...by their stillness become sages, by their movement
kings"*[8] .

> *If there is no other, there will be no I. If there is no I,*
> *there will be none to make distinctions.*

> Chuang Tzu[9]

---

9. Chuang Tzu with Kuo Hsiang's commentary, trans. Fung Yu-lan
(1975), p. 34, 46

A beautiful consequence of this is that the more you resolve the misidentification to temporary matters, the more you *"die the death, that no one ever dies"* and the more you become aware of this complete lack of separate self, the more benevolence and love will spring up towards all creation. After all, what difference is there between your environment and your very own organism? They are just waves dancing at the surface of the ocean. If you are the ocean out of which all things act, it is only natural to feel a universal compassion for all your waves, for everything that *is* and not just for your own body[10].

10. Loy wrote an article elaborating this idea more in-depth (1997): Loving the World as Our Own Body -The Nondualist Ethics of Taoism, Buddhism and Deep Ecology

The World in Action

Part IV

Chapter Sixteen

Just do it!

What to aim for in the all-encompassing, everlasting now?

This is a difficult one. In a world, where you really only have the everlasting now, that is constantly unfolding in ever-changing, fleeting temporality, what are you even supposed to aim for? Let's recall the following paragraph from the section "*you are not temporal*", with the exception that I replaced the word "now" with the Tao. Feel free to mentally replace "the Tao" with words like "I", "God" or "Christ" in a second read through:

One more thing: Trying to contact "the Tao", or the present moment, doesn't make sense. It implies that "the Tao" is not fully present already. That there is something that has to happen first so in some imaginary future now you will be able to access it. However, this future Tao will never arrive - the Tao is here and has been here the whole time. You don't have to learn or to try or to do anything. There is no way to reach something that already is. It is not some specific experience you might have in the future - it is the inherent nature of every experience that you have, now and always. This is one of the greatest paradoxes of them all: the necessity of doing implies the existence of time and some form of change that needs to happen before we can reach the Tao. While not doingwell we would just remain as we are today, wouldn't we? This perfectly illustrates the shortcoming of words in trying to describe universal, eternal consciousness. This is why Sri Ramana Maharshi says: "There is neither creation nor destruction; neither destiny nor free-will; neither path nor achievement; this is the final truth." Any and all of those things would imply that the Tao is not omni-present and timeless and perfect already. We just need to stop resisting and moving away from it. But even that implies the necessity of action again, which is... well... just not true. We are perfect already. Universal consciousness is timeless and inherent to all life already.

There is no doing, no learning, no changing. You are perfect the way you are. You are. And this is all you ever need to be. There is nothing to prove, nowhere to get to and nothing to achieve. However, we need to be very careful not to become nihilistic (*"what does it matter then anyways? Why would I need to get out of bed in the morning?"*). If the resulting feeling is indifference instead of compassion, love and a natural drive, there are probably still unresolved feelings and trauma blocked away. They can keep you from becoming aware of the natural, deep calm and compassion in life. In this case, it's probably better to go back to the section "*Psychological mastery as a prerequisite for spiritual progress*" and perhaps spending more time with the first part of the book and psychological mastery before diving deeper into spiritual topics.

Even though the moment (or the Tao) is always present, you can still learn how to observe, how to resist your present experience less, how to be less captured by the waves and be more fulfilled by the ocean-side of life. You have been given a body and a mind to play the game. Befriend your emotions, know your story and accept your experiences. Bear your responsibility, find a purpose to fulfill and live honorably by the set of values that you feel drawn to. Don't forget to be playful while you're at it. It is in your nature to act, to constantly unfold your potential. *A man cannot live even for a second without performing some sort of action.* True individuality can and will develop the more you are rooted in the whole. It will lead to a natural impulse to act, to be and to do as you see fit.

From a growing presence to oneself, an understanding of what we should do and what we shouldn't do will arise spontaneously. We become creators of our own moral values[1] . The resulting discrimination is important for our own well-being. This is however to be done without judging. Things aren't good or bad, they all have their place in the world. It's more about asking: Is their place in your life? (...*I still wanna see you eat, just not at my table*). What feels good for you? What authentically matches with your needs, wants and dreams? What do(n't) you want to have in your life? This discrimination will greatly benefit from the value exercise laid out in the chapter *A Sense of Identity*.

> "*Discrimination is a prerequisite on the path of spirituality. It distinguishes between truth and untruth. [...]*
> *between the permanent and the impermanent*"

---

1. Maieutique, Perspective 5

Huzur Maharaj Sawan Singh[2]

Creation

"Whoever has the most fun wins"

Origin unknown

The power of thought. Let's say that you have a goal that you want to achieve, like a financial goal regarding income streams or wealth, or a personal goal in a hobby, for your social environment or in your career. Maybe you want to be able to score ten basketball hoops in a row. Or maybe you want to finally stop wearing socks with sandals. What comes first? You set your *mind* to it.

At first, I wanted to write about the *magic* power of thought. That you create the world simply by thinking it. That through the "web of energy" matter has consciousness and mirrors your mind. That a lot of medical issues are a direct consequence of unresolved emotional issues[3]. That the universe will magically grant you all your wishes and support you in your endeavors. Unfortunately, the scientific evidence

---

3. E.g. the highly successful Louise Hay (1984): You can heal your life; or (1998): Heal Your Body A–Z: The Mental Causes for Physical Illness and the Way to Overcome Them.

for this is flimsy, at best. An institute at Princeton specialized in this type of research for 28 years[4]. They conducted experiments in which participants were trying to influence analogue and digital coin flips purely by the power of thought. The results were statistically relevant to indicate *some* influence, but on average only amounted to 2 to 3 coin flips changed out of 10.000[5]. But at the end of the day, this doesn't even matter. We don't need to build this thought on mystic experience or esoterics or quantum physics:

Even if you don't magically create a house simply by thinking about it, the thought of it will always be the first step. And consciousness, the fact of being human, allows you to think about it and then move your hands in a way that will start building the house. Or it will allow you to generate the resources necessary to build a house. Or it will allow you to become aware of the opportunities that are supporting you in owning a house. So technically, we *do* create the world by first thinking of it. Even if in between there are several more steps, like earning the money, buying the plot of land, designing the house etc. At the end of the day, humankind creates its environment. Human impact is so great that most of today's world is directly or indirectly influenced by human thought, word and action at some point. Even remote national parks are influenced by the conscious decision to alter them as little as possible.

So our environment is undoubtedly mirroring our minds, at least on a collective level. Is it really that far-fetched to come to the same conclusion on an individual level? Your physical and social environ-

---

4. E.g. Jahn, Dunne (2005): the PEAR Proposition

5. New York Times (2007): A Princeton Lab on ESP plans to close its doors; online at:

ment, what you own and how you spend your time will certainly tell a great deal about your state of mind, your thoughts and your emotions. Show me your environment and I will show you who you are. I hope the book has so far been empowering enough to understand that this "life mirrors your mind"- thing works both ways. On the one hand, you can clear your mind by cleaning your room; on the other, you can pretty much design your life on a whiteboard. Once you are resilient enough to "tidy up" your emotional turmoil and pull it into the scope of your consciousness, you are free to create the life you want to have. Who and what do you want to have around you? What do you want to spend your time with? What do you want to look like? Failing to think about these questions will not stop you from creating nonetheless. *A man's values are the product of the thinking he has done or failed to do*[6] . A man's *life* is the product of the creating he has done or failed to do! These thoughts are also reflected in the Maieutique perspectives:

"The Being creates the world by thinking it. What you perceive is just a fragment of this immense meditation. Who is aware that he exists as pure being, contemplates the ongoing creation of the world. He sees that the universe is a dream built on a void. The world appears to you as the Eternal's game. This very game which from day to day is yours[7] .

You are a creator. In biblical archetypes, God created the world - which, by the way, is really just a christian way of saying "eternity is constantly unfolding itself in impermanence". We also come across the idea of "man being created in God's image"[8] . Thereby it would only be logical to assume that we also received some of this power

---

6. Branden (1969): The Psychology of Self-Esteem

7. Maieutique Perspective 15

8. Genesis 1:26-28

to create. Some of this power to unfold ourselves in the world. You might have come across manifestation books in this context[9]. I am not the biggest fan of manifestation, especially without working on your character first or without putting a focus on discipline and action. It is oftentimes motivated by misidentification and attachment to temporary things. If you're not attached to the idea of being the rich guy with a nice Ferrari as a status symbol, why would you need to manifest one in the first place? Doesn't trying to manifest a Ferrari imply that you are currently lacking one and therefore increase your current feeling of "not enough"? A realized person doesn't need to be concerned with the fruits of their actions, they can manifest and act for the purpose of acting, for the purpose of simply unfolding themselves.

The world will always stay in balance. You cannot magically "gain" things without working for them. The actual reward will not be the Ferrari in front of your house, but the character, resilience and discipline that you had to acquire to get there. If you find this idea difficult to believe, go research the stories of lottery winners[10]. A multi-million dollar lottery win is rarely delivering a lasting quality of life, and instead drastically increases the chances of bankruptcy, drug overdoses and death by homicide[11]. If you don't put in the work of character

---

9. The most prominent of them probably being "The Secret" by Rhonda Byrne (2006)

10. Very interesting stories on what happens to lottery winners and what can be done about it can be found on Reddit:

11. Studies by scientific standards are hard to find on this topic. An article by Time Magazine tells at least a part of the story: Chan (2016): Here's how winning the lottery makes you miserable.

development, no reward will have any lasting effect on you or your quality of life.

Yes, you *can* manifest your dream job or partner - but you still need to put in the work. Are you skilled in what you do? Are you taking the time and discipline to improve your skill set in your desired field? Does the way you compose yourself make you desirable? If your bonding behavior is full of unhealed and unrecognized trauma-patterns, how can you have a stable relationship? If you are lazy, overweight and spend all your free time on the couch watching movies, "just being yourself" will probably not be too interesting for that model that goes to the gym five days a week. Yes, authenticity is important; but personality is fluid and can be developed to a large degree.

"Get out of your apartment. Meet a member of the opposite sex. Stop the excessive shopping and masturbation. Quit your job. Start a fight. Prove you're alive. If you don't claim your humanity you will become a statistic. You have been warned"

Tyler Durden

Play. Be. Have fun. If you want to go paragliding, go paragliding. If you want to wear socks with sandals, go wear socks with sandals. Just keep in mind that this world will always mirror you. Actions have consequences. If you put in grit, discipline and effort, you shall be rewarded. If you wreak havoc in other people's lives you should not be surprised if the same happens to you. The world will always keep its equilibrium. That doesn't mean that we can't have some fun tipping the scales in one way or another - as long as we remember that it's just a game.

Just don't lose yourself chasing ghosts. Eternity is now. All the goals and riches and perfection in the world won't make you eternally happy, all they can possibly do is slightly raise the share of positive emotions - which we will get used to in no time anyways.

Live life by design, not by default: Goals, purpose & vision

> *"If a man knows not to which port he sails, no wind is favourable."*

Seneca

Throughout this book, awareness has been a key concept, whether in the context of our past, our inner experiences, or our identity. Awareness is just as important when it comes to shaping our general life trajectory. The saying that best illuminated this idea to me was "live your life by design, not by default"[12]. To take charge of one's life instead of being a passenger of chance and fate.

But how do we go about this? How does one live life by design? First, it is critical to become clear about one current or desired main area of development and action. To help find this one single area to focus on, we can revisit the questions from the chapter *A Sense of Identity*. This time, we expand the list with more forward-looking questions. Also consider creating your own questions that best fit your situation:

- What am I dreaming of?

- What is worth suffering for?

- What are milestones that I could reach on the way to that

---

12. Origin unknown

dream?

- What would I have to do to get to these milestones?

- Which actions and habits precisely do I have to build for this path?

- What do I generally want to achieve in life?

- In what kind of situations am I having fun or feeling satisfied?

- What do I want to want?

- What do I want to spend my time with?

- What do I want to work on?

- Am I more interested in things or people?

- What do I look for in a partner?

- What kind of person do I want to be?

So does everyone have an inherent higher purpose that we are naturally drawn to? Honestly, I'm not sure. For the record: Manual labour is just as noble as some fancy "impact-driven" office job, if not more so. Your office job is probably not going to feed people, nor keep societal infrastructure in place. Either way, I think at the core of our purpose are two things: existence and authenticity. Fortunately, a state of pure authenticity and zero resistance naturally comes as a state of action[13].

---

13. This will be discussed in more detail in the chapter "I am non-dual" in the next part of the book.

So I'm merely being pragmatic here: not feeling some sense of purpose or duty in my course of action indicates to me that I am somehow cut off from the natural flow of life. Either way, having something that gives me a feeling of useful contribution to a functioning society simply feels better than aimlessly floating around and being the sum product of what happens to me.

Instead of looking for your one big calling, I think the key task of purpose-finding lies in listening to what is there - your emotions, your history, your dreams, strengths and weaknesses - and then telling the story of what you find. This includes taking decisive action even in the face of uncertainty. The act of picking something and sticking to it for a set timeframe is so much more important than *what* you pick. Through action and failure you will be able to sharpen your understanding of the path that feels most natural to you and that you feel most drawn to. Hesitation and following five different possible options at once will lead you nowhere. As the saying goes, "A man who chooses two rabbits catches neither". I had a year where I didn't prioritize between piano, paragliding, work, writing this book, sports, relationships and self-education. Dancing on seven different weddings at the same time prevented me from making actual meaningful progress in any one of the areas.

One more thing: Be careful not to sacrifice the things that you want (serenity, peace and love) for the thing that is supposed to get them for you (success)[14] . Striving too fiercely for a different future state of being always implies a discontent with current affairs, thus preventing you from finding peace in the present. I don't think it's about *reaching* your purpose. I think it's more about getting comfortable with

---

14. Credits to Chris Williamson's Podcast "Modern Wisdom" for this idea

striving for it. This "continuous state of development" relates a lot to discipline and becoming comfortable with stress in a controlled environment. This will help us accept the natural challenges that occur in the river of life in a more calm and resilient manner[15].

Purpose, passion or just a commitment to discipline?

We are one and a half years into the reign of Mirco the fourth. I'm on a plane to Portugal for my summer holidays. I notice the guy to my right is reading Eastern spiritual texts. Not the Eat Pray Love type where you go to Bali to fall in love. More the type where you spend thirty years in a monastery to not be distracted by worldly matters. He doesn't look like the type of guy to spend more than an hour in a monastery though. Never judge a book by its cover I guess. Can I judge a guy by his book though? I strike up a conversation with him, which turns out to be a wonderful decision. As much as he was spiritually interested, he was determined in a business context. He worked in Swiss investment banking, earning a buttload of money. He wasn't your run of the mill finance bro though. For him, it was a conscious decision how he wanted to spend his time in the present and the future. "Just think about what you want to do, make a plan and go do it. Forget everything else". Neither the mindset nor the thought were really new for me. Nonetheless, it was exactly what I needed to hear. Forget societal restraints, my own limiting beliefs or monetization. Forget what people expect of me! Forget what I think I can't do! What do I want to do? What would I have the most fun

---

15. Feel free to revisit the ice bathing chapter for this thought.

doing? Which path of action would be most aligned to my thoughts and emotions? I love thinking about the big questions in life, be it from a perspective of psychology, philosophy or spirituality. I have fun discussing them. Why not just write it all up for once? Maybe in a book?

The longer I thought about it, the more I loved the idea. In the following months, I started collecting potential chapters to include. It took months because I only spent about one or two hours per month on it. A long subway ride here, waiting before a doctor's visit there, nothing too urgent. I had a reason for taking my time. Back in elementary school, I skipped a year. Supposedly it was the year in which they taught you to write essays. People told me that my creative writing sucked, because I had missed that year. Being roughly three years younger, I also lacked the emotional maturity to match my peers' essays in subsequent years. So all my life I had been stuck with this belief that my writing is terrible. Before I could actually start writing, I had to realize that this was complete nonsense. More and more instances from the last few years came to my mind, where I loved writing, especially in the context of resolving or creating experiences. The long letter after the Christmas incident. Writing down my thoughts and feelings after arguments. Writing short stories as a way of flirting with a muse. Writing love poems. The surprisingly good feedback on my last-minute bachelor thesis. I love writing!

Now all that was left to do was sit down and write my thoughts down. Piece of cake right? Uh... no. Not really. Motivation is all nice and well but it comes and goes. I could only write when I actually felt like writing and had the time to do it. That would leave me rather vulnerable to... well... not writing at all. Discipline eats motivation for breakfast[16]. I

---

16. Credits to a conversation between Jocko Willink and Chris
   Williamson

needed to get to a point where it no longer required my conscious decision. To a point where I just sit down and write. No questions asked.

Forming new habits in an existing time schedule can be difficult. Mountains, piano, friends, work, sports. I had existing networks and failsafes in place to keep me in this structure. People asking me to join here and there. I had difficulties saying no. Play table tennis on a Tuesday night? Sure, why not. Hang out on Friday night? Absolutely! It might prevent me from falling into dark rabbit holes. It also prevented me from building significant new structures, however. I somehow needed to first strip things away that were not absolutely essential to me[17]. Sure, being playful and spending time with friends and in nature is important. But something needed to change to make room for a new habit - my commitment to writing.

Sometimes, changing yourself, your thoughts or your mindset isn't enough. Sometimes you have to collect new experiences or change your environment. Environments are linked to habits. If you start playing games every time you sit down at your computer, it becomes increasingly difficult to change your path of action on the same computer, at the same desk, in the same room. Interrupting habit patterns can be a helpful support structure to learn new habits or get rid of old ones. If you wanted to radically change the nature of your computer use, you could for example use a different colored desk and position it elsewhere in your living space. If you wanted to stop the half-conscious phone checks that so many of us are doing these days, you could put your phone in a different pocket. Your hand might reach into the original pocket, but it will not find a phone to pull out and check. On the other hand (literally), the motion is just not as established yet. Therefore, it would require a more conscious effort to

---

17. Reading tip: McKeown (2014): Essentialism. The Disciplined Pursuit of Less.

pull out your phone and check it. These links also work with sensory and acoustic input. If you always listen to the same playlist when having sex, listening to the same playlist for studying is just going to put you in a rather awkward position at the library.

For me, getting a new desk or changing up my playlists didn't quite do the trick. Instead, I moved to Paris for half a year. That did the trick. In an entirely new environment with a new city, no friends and no inbuilt habits, I could pretty much design my days outside of work on a whiteboard. Within weeks I found lovely people to spend time with, a routine that fulfilled all my needs and still had plenty of time left to do my writing.

Chapter Seventeen

The chicken-egg conundrum

Responsibility or the antithesis that the egg came first

Out of the night that covers me,
Black as the pit from pole to pole,
I thank whatever gods may be
For my unconquerable soul.

In the fell clutch of circumstance
I have not winced nor cried aloud.
Under the bludgeonings of chance
My head is bloody, but unbowed.

Beyond this place of wrath and tears

Looms but the Horror of the shade,
And yet the menace of the years
Finds and shall find me unafraid.

It matters not how strait the gate,
How charged with punishments the scroll,
I am the master of my fate,
I am the captain of my soul.

Invictus
By William Ernest Henley

U sually, your model of the world shapes your actions. In turn, these will build the experiences you have, which will influence your model of the world again. Putting it together in a graph looks like this:

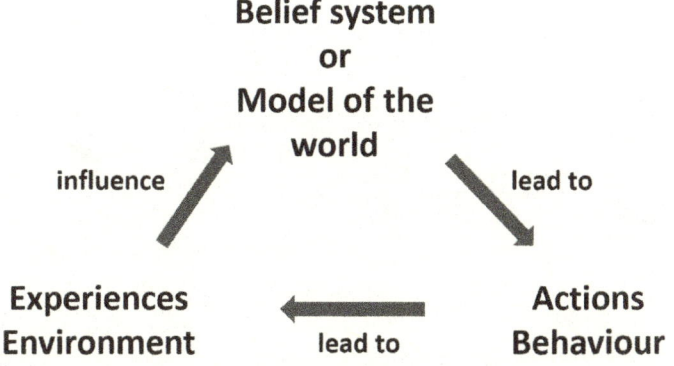

Of course these directions are not entirely sharp. There are other dependencies in opposite directions, too. For example:

- Your model of the world will directly influence how you assess, filter and perceive your experiences, independent of how they objectively are. If you buy a certain car, you will suddenly see the same model all over the place. Whereas before, you had never really seen it before.

- Your actions can also directly shape your beliefs, independent of what these actions lead you to experience. If you start going to the gym regularly, you will feel capable of building a new habit, mostly independent of the experiences you have at the gym.

- Your environment is also directly linked to how you behave. A change of environment will easily lead to a change of action, without any modification of your model of the world or your belief system.

Let's rearrange the graph a little, to group the *outside* on the left (experiences and environment), and the *inside* on the right (beliefs and actions).

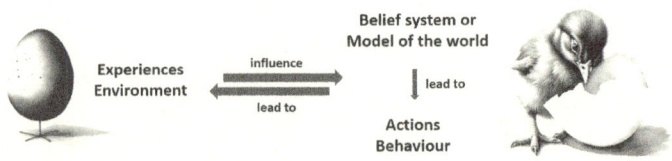

Now, if you want change in life, how do you go about it? The way this book is structured is the way I personally learned it and needed to learn it: The chicken comes first. A change in beliefs leads to a change of behavior, which changes the environment, the feedback from the world and the experience of life. This increases quality in life.

However, there is another way to go about it[1]. It is to start with the egg, not the chicken. You could radically ignore Freudian psychoanalytic shenanigans and with it, the past as much as any reasoning for your present-day behavior. You can skip all that and go straight to changing the experiences you have and the environment you find yourself in. If you look at the circle, it can essentially have the same effect just the other way around: experiences and environments influence behavior, which leads to changes in belief and perception, leading to an overall change in well-being and quality of life.

This can be advantageous: a real-world experience is more convincing than just telling yourself something. Let's look at two examples:

The first is an approach that psychologist Milton Erickson[2] took with a suicidal patient who felt deeply unattractive: Erickson advised her to "prank" her favorite work colleague at the water fountain by using the unfavorable gap between her teeth to spit water at him: *"He was startled and the consequences were expectable... he says, 'You little bitch, I'm going to KISS you for that!' She turned and ran and he ran after her caught her...[sic] two months later they were married"*[3]. The experience enabled her to change her belief system and consequently,

---

1. Gordon, Meyers-Anderson (1981): Phoenix: Therapeutic Patterns of Milton H. Erickson, p. 85ff

2. Milton Erickson is more well-known for his work around hypnosis. He had however very interesting approaches with changing belief systems and experiences of his patients that didn't make use of hypnosis

3. Gordon, Meyers-Anderson (1981): Phoenix: Therapeutic Patterns of Milton H. Erickson, p. 131

her following behavior: she had undeniable proof of being attractive. Even more so: Something previously considered unattractive - the gap in her teeth - was essential in achieving this attraction and outcome.

The second example showcases one of Frank Farrelly's methods in his *provocative therapy*. He often proposed nonsensical explanations for clients' problems to deliver the message: "*To hell with psychogenesis. Just deal with the fact!*" Among others, the explanations given were the following:

- "*There are some mysteries in life that will never be revealed*"

- "*Obviously you had crooked chromosomes to start off with...*"

- "*I don't know if you are immoral, weak, or just lazy*"

- "*You've probably got an unresolved oedipal complex - your mother tried to seduce you?*"

Once patients realized that they didn't necessarily *need* to understand everything, they were often able to make relevant changes in their life and behavior[4].

How you go about it is up to your personal preference. I *wanted* to understand my past, my story and why I acted the way I did. But you will know best, what is right for you and how you can go about it. Much better than me or anyone else. This book is just here to help you differentiate between roads and impassable wilderness. But it is upon you to choose the roads to take.

Even if you do start with the chicken: all of the therapy and belief-system work will only prove effective once it is realized in action.

---

4. Farrelly, Brandsma (1981): Provocative Therapy, p. 73ff.

You don't become confident by shouting affirmations in the mirror, but by having a stack of undeniable proof that you are who you say you are. Outwork your self doubt.

Alex Hormozi

I think Alex oversees the positive impact that mirror work and affirmations can have. He is right about this though: it won't be worth much, unless you build evidence for your beliefs in the way you interact with the world. How else are you going to believe yourself? This is in line with how you can measure progress in therapy. Oftentimes, you do not look at the experiences of a patient, but rather their outside. Do they have friends, a job or a relationship? Do they function in daily life, performing tasks and activities? Are they able to build meaningful connections?

The belief-system chicken

Let's ignore the belief system-chicken for now and look at possible eggtions to take regarding your experiences and environment:

Think about your input

What do you feed your senses? What is the visual, acoustic or nutritional input that you have day in, day out? TV, "news", porn, alcohol, sugar, tobacco, other drugs? Well then it shouldn't come as a surprise to you that life feels sluggish and tedious. If you cut all of that out by tomorrow, you would probably be completely overwhelmed from all the emotional and sensory input that you are suddenly aware of. I think it's a gradual process: the more I can become aware of my inner experience, the less I need all these drugs. The less I use these drugs, the more I come alive. I was prone to be addicted to plenty of things: tobacco, alcohol, games, chips, you name it. Either I was fully addicted, or I had to be careful in my way of handling things.

If you don't know where to start, focus on the basics: Eight hours of sleep per night, early morning sunlight exposure and at least two liters of water per day. Add some exercise a few times per week as well as food that contains less sugar and a few more nuts and vegetables and you have a solid structure. Stick to at least half of these for three to six months and then see how you feel. It sounds ridiculously simple, but complex problems don't necessarily require complex solutions.

Think about your environment

Make things that you want to do convenient. How can you achieve this? Let's take going to the gym as an example. You could find a gym that is closest to your home. You could always have your gym bag on hand and ready to go. You could leave sports shoes near the front door to remind you. You could find a gym buddy to go together with. After all, explaining to someone else that you're *"not feeling it today, you'll just go tomorrow"* is much more difficult. What does an environment look like that gets you to do what you want to do? If you want to study, maybe just go to the library and, just for an hour, sit next to 100 people studying. Then see what you are inclined to do. My best guess is you will start studying as well.

Get in situations where you *have* to act the way you want to. Remember when, at the beginning of this book, I didn't get jack shit done in Vienna, and moved away and did landscaping for six months? I had accidentally put myself in a position where the cure happened automatically. I *had* to get up in the morning and be a productive member of society. I mean, if I utterly failed in getting *anything* done for two years and then moved away to take a job of manual labor and *still* failed, where else could I go? I had failed at knowledge work and I would have failed at manual labor. In my - luckily rather unimaginative - mind, there was no going lower than being unable to perform both types of work in the world. I *had* to get up and go to work. I had no other choice. Frequently, I would play on the computer or join rooftop parties until 1 or 2 am, but when my alarm rang at 6, I would get up and drive to work, no matter how tired I was.

This goes the other way, too. Make the things that you don't want to do inconvenient in advance. Place them out of reach and out of sight. Lock them away. Give yourself hurdles that interrupt your destructive habit patterns. Don't hang out with the people that are linked to behaviors that you want to get rid of.

Chapter Eighteen

Panta Rhei

Part I
A state of authenticity and congruence

Sticking feathers up your butt does not make you a chicken.

Tyler Durden

There is one key aspect for *the world in action* that we haven't explicitly discussed yet: Authenticity. What does it mean? How does it relate to the concepts in this book? And why is it so important?

The entire second part of this book, *The Self in Flow*, is directed at achieving authentic awareness and expression of inner experience. Nonetheless, there are a few insights from parts 3 and 4 that are essential for a holistic approach to authenticity.

Carl Rogers uses the concept of congruence[1] . It's what he calls *"a matching of experience, awareness and communication"*. He uses infants as an example. When they are hungry, their awareness is filled with the experience of being hungry, and their communication is aligned accordingly.

This might necessitate the absence of an analytical mind, like in the case of infants. You experience, you feel, you express. However, your mind and your thoughts are also just a part of *that experience* that you can become aware of and express. As Rogers then hypothesizes, this congruence subsequently leads to better relationships:

The greater the congruence of experience awareness and communication on the part of one individual, the more the ensuing relationship will involve a tendency toward...

- *reciprocal communication with a quality of increasing congruence,*

- *a more mutually accurate understanding of the communications,*

- *improved psychological adjustment and functioning in both parties,*

- *mutual satisfaction in the relationship.*

So, in simpler terms, if we are aware of what we feel and if we can then somehow communicate what we are aware of, this will directly lead to better relationships. This is why I focused on social connection so little throughout the book, despite its importance for well-being. I believe that the learnings leading towards authenticity are a wonderful

---

1. Rogers (1961): On Becoming a Person

foundation for building meaningful human connection. They hopefully empower you to become more aware of your inner experiences as well as to express them fearlessly. I have had people open up to me with their darkest, deepest demons shortly after meeting them. Telling me about their addictions and diagnoses and drug abuse. Even in a professional environment. And it only led to building and strengthening a bond. I considered them to be more trustworthy and more likeable.

So then why don't we do this anyways? Why isn't this the case already in interpersonal communication and relationships? Rogers goes on to identify the main roadblock for this: self-defense. Self-defense against the lingering possibility of threat or rejection. Playing into social expectations. If you're hiding something or if it's just a persona that you are playing, then you can always fall back on the fact that they didn't see the "real you" and only rejected whatever image you played for them. However, as with all things dual, this has a flip side: if playing a persona leads you to being successful or desired, you won't be able to feel connected to this. At best, it's applause for the role you play, but not true appreciation for who you are, since no one can really see the real you[2].

We always have a choice: do we take risks and communicate congruently? Or do we resort back to whatever behavior we think is expected of us. Not realizing that this is detrimental for all parties involved, independent of the outcome it leads to. *Rogers writes: "It seems to me that it is the taking or not taking of this risk which determines whether a given relationship becomes more and more mutually therapeutic or whether it leads in a disintegrative direction".*

The further we resolve the misidentification laid out in the chapter "Who am I not", the less we need to feel threatened by inevitable

---

2. Credits to Chris Williamson for this thought.

changes in our life and reputation. It is our thirst for the impossible that makes things difficult: To keep steady what is unsteady. To make eternal what is temporal. To make possible what is impossible. It is an unhealthy resistance to the natural flow of all things in life. *Panta Rhei*. Sooner or later, your reputation or your social standing is going to fade anyways, no matter what you do. Some people try to fight this by building their legacy. It might remain after their death but it is a short-sighted endeavor. The greatest heroes of our time will be forgotten in a few generations or centuries at the latest. We are not our car or our job as much as we are not our reputation. So stop hiding that quirky, odd human that we all are inside. Forget adapting yourself to societal expectations. *I say never be complete. I say stop being perfect. I say let's evolve. Let the chips fall where they may*[3].

We have these stuck-up ideas of who we are, how we should be perceived and who we are supposed to be. If we let go of all of that, the need for self-defense against congruence disappears. After all, what is left to defend once you realize that your reputation is not *you*? Oddly enough, this attitude radiates illuminating confidence. It shows that there isn't anything that you consider to be a threat or hurtful rejection. Maybe you finally realized that we are the all-singing, all-dancing crap of the world.

Part II
The Philosopher's Stone

---

3. A quote from our beloved friend, Tyler Durden

For the last section, let's go down the rabbit hole of alchemy. Alchemy? I thought alchemists were just early chemists, messing around with strange ingredients on a fruitless quest? Well, let's have a closer look! Traditionally, alchemists were attempting to create the philosopher's stone. It was supposed to bring eternal life and transmute cheaper metals into gold. According to Wikipedia, achieving this feat was thought to result in the perfection of body and soul.

Unknown to many, the idea that the philosopher's stone, the *lapis philosophorum,* was more than just the result of a chemical process, came up as early as the fourteenth century[4]. Gerhard Dorn, a Belgian mid-16th century alchemist was probably the first in the west to seriously elaborate on the psychological side to this search for truth[5]. In his *de philosophia speculativa* he exclaims: "*Transform yourselves into living philosophical stones!*"[6] The whole thing is a psychic synthesis as much as it is a chemical process!

For this transformation into "living philosophical stones" he proposes three phases. Each of these phases consists of a union of opposites of some sort. The aim to unite opposites is deeply woven into the historic fabric of alchemy. Alchemists understood the necessity of overcoming duality on the way to "*healing all ills*" surprisingly well[7].

---

4. Jung (1955): Mysterium Coniunctionis, p. 676

5. most of Dorn's writings in this direction can be found in the theatrum chemicum, published by Zetzner in 1602

6. Dorn (1602): De philosophia speculativa, p. 239. Quoted in Jung (1944): Psychology and Alchemy, p. 148.

7. Refer to the chapter "I am not dual" for an in-depth discussion of the principle of union of opposites

The first of these three unions is the *unio mentalis* - a mental union. It refers to the marriage of intellect or reason with emotions. This union leads to the ability to rationally become aware of and understand one's emotional currents and turmoils. It comes with a significant increase in maturity and self-knowledge. Alchemists considered the self to be more of "*a substance hidden in the body, identical with the image of god*" and less of the fragile, temporal ego-self that we so desperately hold on to. While it still treats the self as a separate entity, it reflects the aspect of immanence that we discussed in the chapter "Who am I": *I am the one who is immanent in all*" or "*it is Christ who lives in me*".

The *unio mentalis* also requires an overcoming of the body of some sort. Even though emotions are also stored in the body, one first needs to ignore animalistic needs for food, safety or procreation long enough to balance and unite *ratio* (reason)and *eros* (emotions). Completing this first phase does not yet result in a wise man, but simply a mental disciple of wisdom. "*Its reality is mere potential*", Jung writes. To realize this potential and to bring out the wise man, a second union needs to be achieved: that of the *unio mentalis* with the physical body. Integrating the body is step two. To act out this previously achieved union of reason and feelings. To move the body in accordance with inner experience. To express what one feels and what one is aware of in speech, gesture and movement. This hopefully feels familiar! It is the alchemist's version of Carl Rogers' approach to congruence. It is also essentially the ideal outcome of the first two parts of this book: becoming aware of our inner experience and using our body to fluently express what we are aware of.

Dorn also had very specific thoughts about the third conjunction: he dreamed of uniting the whole man with *unus mundus* - one world. To erase the border between yourself and the world! Or better yet, to realize that it was never there in the first place! Jung thinks that Dorn used *unus mundus* to refer to a potential, unified world: "*the potential world of the first day of creation, when nothing was yet 'in actu,' i.e., divided into two and many, but was still one. [...]. The eternal ground of all empirical being*"[8].

This sounds to me like he is describing the universal eternal observer. The Tao. What Buddha described as non-composed, non-inflamed, or as the one who has not come to existence. The third stage also sounds familiar, doesn't it? It's obviously the marriage of the observer and the observed that was the culmination of the third part of the book - "The World in Flow". As a quick reminder: observer and observed are simply two sides of the same coin. There is only one thing - observation. Existence. Love.

So what does it lead to then? Peterson summarized Jung's writings in this regard with the following sentence: "*At the highest level of psychological integration, there is no difference between you and what you experience*"[9]. This has practical implications: If your room is disorganized, is it your room that is disorganized, or your experience? If there is no difference between you and what you experience, then is it your room that is messy, or is it *you*? It's a solid basis for taking responsibility not just for your body, but for your *experience*. For everything that is happening around you. For taking charge in your life and structuring your experience in a desirable way. It's also a wonderful foundation for developing a universal compassion for your entire experience, not just for your own body or personal ego.

---

8. Jung (1955): Mysterium coniunctionis, p. 760

9. The Jordan B. Peterson Podcast: 147. Carl Rogers (Humanism & Phenomenology)

When identity is simply experience, it also has theoretical implications: When I achieve the highest degree of union, overcoming all duality and erasing the border between myself and the world, then who I am, what I am, what I want... all of these questions become meaningless, at least temporarily. All that is left is my perception. Pure experience. A living philosopher's stone! I am he who is. I am that I am[10].

10. Exodus 3:14, English Standard Version

About the Author

Fred has always been curious about psychology and philosophy. He grew up in southern Germany in and out of different (boarding) schools before finishing school at the age of 15 in New Zealand. In his early years in university he felt rather lost, before a failed relationship led him to work through the remnants of his past and to search for peace and purpose in life. The answers and questions he found in the next decade in therapy, in researching the topic of trauma, and in spiritual endeavours are captured in this book. Nowadays he works in climate change advisory in Vienna, having consulted some of the biggest companies in Europe in environmental matters. Outside of work, he loves paragliding, playing the piano and writing (obviously!).

If you want to chat or share your thoughts about the book, feel free to drop a line at fred.pantarhei@gmail.com or hit him up on X at pantarhei68

Made in the USA
Las Vegas, NV
02 October 2024